The Tree
of the Knowledge
of Good and Evil

Translated from the French
Original title: L'ARBRE DE LA CONNAISSANCE
DU BIEN ET DU MAL

Prosveta S.A – B.P.12 – 83601 Fréjus CEDEX (France)

ISSN 0763-2738
ISBN 2-85566-775-5
édition originale: ISBN 2-85566-211-7

Omraam Mikhaël Aïvanhov

The Tree
of the Knowledge
# of Good and Evil

4th edition

Izvor Collection — No. 210

P R O S V E T A

By the same author:

(Translated from the French)

Izvor Collection

TABLE OF CONTENTS

Readers are reminded that Omraam Mikhaël Aïvanhov's teaching was exclusively oral. His published works have been compiled from stenographic notes or electronic recordings of his lectures.

Chapter One

THE TWO TREES OF PARADISE

For thousands of years human beings have tried to understand how the world began and how evil and its attendant ills came into this world. The explanations they found were often presented in the form of myths, and this is why the sacred scriptures of all religions contain symbolical accounts, which can be understood only if we have the key to their interpretation. The Christian tradition, for instance, has adopted the account given by Moses in the Book of Genesis, but does this mean that Christians really understand it?

Let us look, first of all, at what Moses says. On the sixth day of creation God made man and woman and put them in the midst of all kinds of animals and plants in a garden called Eden. Two of the trees in this garden are mentioned specifically: the tree of life, and the tree of the knowledge of good and evil—and it is the latter that has since become particularly notorious. God forbade Adam and Eve to eat the fruits of this tree, and as long as they obeyed him they lived happily in the midst of abundance. But then the serpent came and persuaded Eve to taste the fruit of the tree of the knowledge of good and evil, and Eve in turn persuaded Adam, with the result that God drove them out of paradise. This is the substance of the story, and we shall come back to certain aspects of it in a moment.

A great many people have gone in search of this earthly paradise, believing that it must have been in India, America, or Africa, but of course no one has ever found it. The Garden of Eden was certainly on earth, but what exactly is meant by earth? As you will soon see, the whole account is symbolic. Of course, I cannot explain every detail to you; that would be impossible, for the whole question of the first man and woman is too vast, but let me begin by telling you about the two trees, the tree of life and the tree of the knowledge of good and evil.

As you know, when Adam and Eve lived in paradise they were allowed to eat the fruit of all the trees in the garden with one exception, that of the tree of the knowledge of good and evil. But what you do not know is that the fruit of this tree is the symbol of all those forces that the first man and woman were still incapable of controlling, transforming, and using. This is why God told them: 'The time will come when you will be allowed to eat this fruit, but at the moment you are still too weak. If you eat it, the forces it contains will kill you, and you will die.' The words, 'you will die' we should understand to mean 'your state of consciousness will be changed.' This changed state of consciousness is indicated in Genesis, but it has not always been understood. Genesis says that when Adam and Eve were living happily in paradise, 'they were both naked and were not ashamed.' Later, after eating the forbidden fruit, 'the eyes of both were opened and they knew that they were naked; and they sewed fig leaves together and made themselves aprons.' This sudden awareness of their nakedness shows that there had been a change within them.

The tree of life represents the unity of life, life as it is before it is polarized, before there is either good or evil. The tree of life is a realm that transcends good and evil. The tree of knowledge, on the other hand, represents the world of polarization, a realm in which we are subject to the alternation of day and night, joy and sorrow, and so on. These two trees therefore are not simply phenomena of the vegetable kingdom, they are realms of the universe, or states of mind. God forbade Adam and Eve to eat the fruit of the tree of the knowledge of good and evil because he did not want them to enter the realm of polarization. Why this prohibition? Was it simply a whim on God's part? No. Was this tree useless then? No again. God does not create anything useless. A tree that produced fruit that no one could eat or make use of in any way would be contrary to divine wisdom, for divine wisdom never creates something unless it is useful.

There were beings who were capable of eating the fruit of the tree of the knowledge of good and evil without harm to themselves, but Adam and Eve were not yet ready to do so. The contact with the astringent forces contained in this fruit would have caused the subtle matter of their bodies to congeal and solidify. And in fact, this is exactly what happened. Tradition speaks of a 'fall', and the word 'fall' symbolizes their passage from a subtle state of matter to a state that was more opaque. After eating the forbidden fruit, Adam and Eve were more densely material, and it is this materialization that is expressed in the words 'they knew that they were naked.' Before their act of disobedience they were already naked, but they were clothed in light; afterwards they saw that they had lost their robes of light, and they suddenly felt ashamed and tried to hide.

After eating the forbidden fruit, Adam and Eve continued to live physically, but they died to their higher state of consciousness. They were driven out of paradise (which is the symbol of this higher consciousness), and angels with flaming swords guarded the entrance. What do we mean when we say that Adam and Eve were exiled to earth? The paradise from which they were banished was an 'earthly paradise'; what was the difference then between the earth on which they already lived and that to which they were banished? The Cabbalah teaches that the earth exists in seven forms, and it gives the name and the attributes of each, from the densest to the subtlest, and it was from the subtlest form of earth that the first man and woman were banished.

What do we really know about the earth? If you think about it, you will have to admit that we know very little. According to initiatic science, the earth has an etheric double which surrounds it like a luminous atmosphere. It is this subtle, etheric double that is the true earth spoken of in Genesis, the earth as it was when it came from the hands of God. The true earth is not the solid, condensed ground on which we live. The true earth is the etheric earth. It was on this earth—which we call paradise—that God placed the first human beings. It was here that they lived in the radiant, luminous bodies I spoke of earlier, and they knew neither suffering, nor sickness, nor death.

Paradise still exists. Did you know that? It has never ceased to exist. Although we cannot see it, it is all around us as a material reality, but a reality that exists on the subtle, etheric plane of matter. And the tree of eternal life still stands in paradise and still produces the elements that constituted the nourishment of our first parents. They lived in and were nourished by this etheric substance of the earth; it was this substance that gave light and purity to their lives. Of course, as I have already said, the tree of life was not actually a tree; it was a current that flowed through this region from the sun. Adam and Eve were nourished by the sun's rays. The tree of life is the sun.

Human beings are constructed in exactly the same way today as when they were first created; they still have the innate capacity to receive the sun's rays, to eat once again the fruits of the tree of life—that is, they still have the ability to turn back to God. Each religion has its own language and its own way of expressing things, but all religions speak of this reintegration in God, of this turning back to the prime cause. With different words they all speak of the same reality.

And now we come to the question: what is the tree of the knowledge of good and evil? This tree also represents a current that flowed through paradise, but a current of a very different sort which put human beings in contact with the densest form of the earth. God told Adam and Eve to be content to explore the realms of the tree of life. The time was not yet ripe for them to leave this region of light and to go down to study the roots of creation. That was for a later stage. They should not try to know everything all at once. Since this second tree existed, there was no question of eliminating it, any more than one can eliminate one's intestines, or liver, or spleen. For just as there are two regions in the universe, there are two regions in man: a higher region which corresponds to the tree of life and a lower region in which are the roots of creation and which corresponds to the tree of the knowledge of good and evil.

The fruit of the tree of the knowledge of good and evil contained such powerful astringent elements (representing the current of *coagula*) that Adam and Eve could not withstand their effect. God knew that these currents would immediately change their state of consciousness, and, as we have seen, this is precisely what happened. On contact with this astringent current, their bodies changed, lost their luminosity, and began to become opaque and more densely material. By forbidding them to eat this fruit— that is, to explore this current and experiment with these natural forces—God wanted to shield them from suffering, sickness, and death (death of the physical body, of course, not of the spirit, for they were created immortal). But they ate the fruit, and as a result they died to their first luminous state and became alive to a state of darkness and density. Then they had to leave paradise, this etheric realm of light and joy, and descend to the lower levels of earth; and it is on this same level of earth that we live today, for we too have left the earth of our first homeland.

Now what about the serpent who tempted Eve? Who or what was this clever creature who talked so persuasively? The serpent is a very profound and comprehensive symbol which is found in all religions. Initiates of every era have always had to deal with the serpent, even though they may choose not to talk about it openly. The serpent symbolizes many realities which on the surface seem very different: the Kundalini force, or evil, or the devil, or the magic agent through which all things flow and are carried from heaven to earth and from earth to heaven.

For an initiate, the serpent is not only a symbol of evil. True, it has this lower aspect of darkness, but it also has a higher aspect of light. It is the magic agent that is capable of transmitting both good and evil. The serpent is what Eliphas Levi called 'astral light'. It can be impregnated with impurities—in which case its effects are harmful—just as it can be suffused with the

luminous thoughts of saints and prophets, which
it carries aloft to the very throne of God. The
serpent therefore is luminous in its upper half and
dark in its lower half. The Zohar (Book of
Splendour) speaks of the symbol of a white,
luminous head which, when reflected in the black
pit of opaque matter, appears as a dark head of
frightful aspect. This is God's shadow. But I
prefer to keep these things for later, when you are
better prepared to understand them. The serpent
or dragon therefore symbolizes this magic agent,
which fills the whole universe, from earth to the
heavens, and is the vehicle of both good and bad
emanations.

If you are familiar with the Tarot you will
know that the fifteenth major trump represents
the devil. Stanislas de Guaita understood the
profound significance of this card. He also wrote
a commentary on a symbolic drawing which
depicts two faces: above is the luminous, radiant
face of a victorious, all-powerful initiate, and
reflected below it, as though in a mirror, is the
image of the devil, a hideous, depraved being
with a face contorted by a devouring rage. The
two together form a single reality as though they
were two triangles linked together; not
intertwined as in the Seal of Solomon ✡ , but
joined at the base ⧖ . This figure signifies that the
devil and the luminous magical agent represent

two levels of one and the same reality. And this can also be seen in human beings: the lower part of their being is unclean and repugnant; the upper part is beautiful and divine. It all depends on the forces they work with, the level of consciousness on which they dwell, and the elements they handle.

The serpent of Genesis therefore represents a current that arises from the earth and ascends to great heights. In the higher reaches it is pure and luminous, and in the lower regions it is obscure and repellent. In any case, we know that it was at home in the Garden of Eden, for it was there that Eve met it. Eve was very curious by nature. She wanted to know exactly what this tree of the knowledge of good and evil was, but as she was afraid to go too near, she began by studying it from a distance. Little by little, however, devoured by curiosity, she moved closer, and as she gazed at it, without daring to touch it, she became more and more aware of the voice of the serpent—that is, of the current that rose from the earth and spoke with such intelligence: 'Ah, but there are many things you do not know yet. You should come and learn from us, for our knowledge is very great.'

Now I must tell you that the serpent was not a single entity. It was an egregor, a coalescence of beings that God had created long before he created human beings; a generation of angels, archangels, and divinities who had been sent by God to work with the fire, metals, and crystals that exist in the depths of the earth. Their mission was to prepare and perfect the riches that lie beneath the surface of the earth, and once this was done, to return to heaven. This is what tradition tells us; I am not making it up. (Sometimes I embroider the traditional stories a little or add some dialogue to make them more alive, but I never invent anything.) So, as I say, tradition tells us that God had created these luminous beings, a whole hierarchy of angels and archangels, and that once their mission was accomplished they were supposed to return to their Creator. However, some of them allowed themselves to be influenced by the life they experienced below and chose not to return to the Lord. This is what is known as the revolt of the angels. They did not rebel while they were in heaven; they rebelled when they were far away from God.

God did not threaten the rebellious angels with death or destruction. He simply said: 'Stay where you are then. You will certainly learn a great deal, and when you are sick of a life of obscurity and constraint you may come back. You will always be welcome.' Yes, such is God's love that he allows even his most debased creatures to return to him. If God truly is love, how could he refuse forever to welcome sinners who want to return to his embrace? Such a refusal would be a terrible cruelty, and it is not possible for God to be cruel. Even demons can return to God, for he is absolute love. You must not think that demons are happy in the life they have chosen, for they are not. But although they suffer, their pride prevents them from turning back to God. The door is always open, however, and as soon as they repent and stop persecuting human beings, they will be restored to their place in heaven, and Lucifer will once again be the archangel of light. A traditional account of the fall tells us that when Lucifer was precipitated into the pit with his cohort of rebellious angels, a great emerald fell from his crown, and this emerald was carved out to form the holy Grail, the cup in which the blood of Christ was saved. What is the relationship between Lucifer and Christ? What do they have to do with each other?

But let us get back to the serpent. As I have already told you, the serpent symbolizes all those spirits, those intelligent, highly evolved beings who possessed immense knowledge but who severed their ties with God. Indeed, it was thanks to their great knowledge that they succeeded in seducing Eve by promising to initiate her into their arcana. Genesis says that Eve ate the apple, but what is so terrible about eating an apple? Everyone eats apples. Yes, but it is the symbolic aspect that interests us, for the apple represents a body of knowledge that was still unknown to Adam and Eve. The serpent told Eve: 'God has forbidden you to eat the fruit of this tree because he knows that if you do so you will be as powerful as he is, and he does not want that. He warned you that you would die, but that is not true. On the contrary, you will live and will learn many things that are still unknown to you.' And Eve succumbed to the temptation, and it was then, according to the Cabbalah, that she conceived her first child. This was Eve's first initiation, and she was so thrilled that she went and told Adam about this wonderful new experience. Until then neither of them knew anything about such things.

Now it is important to know that the Biblical account can be interpreted in many different ways, for the Garden of Eden with its two trees, symbolizes a reality that exists not only in the universe at large but in every human being. In one form or another, men and women continue to taste the fruits either of the tree of life or of the tree of knowledge in their own physical bodies, for our bodies symbolize the Garden of Eden. The tree of the knowledge of good and evil existed in Adam and Eve from the beginning, but never having tasted its fruits, they knew nothing of its properties. Their first initiation therefore was this contact with natural forces of which they were ignorant. The entities that constituted the egregor that we call the serpent were both male and female, and tradition has it that Adam ate the forbidden fruit after being initiated by a female demon called Lilith, whereas Eve was initiated by a male demon called Samaël. From that time on, therefore, Eve went one way and Adam another. Their unity as a couple was destroyed.

It was at this stage that the forces of astringency began their work of coagulation, and although Adam and Eve had never been ashamed of their nudity while their bodies were made of light, now that they had lost their light and become densely material they began to feel shame. This is why the Bible says that they hid themselves amongst the trees of the garden. But how could they hide themselves? No one can hide from God.

You must not think that God was angry with them when he found that they had eaten the forbidden fruit. Why should he be? Perhaps you think that it would be only normal for him to be angry since Adam and Eve had disobeyed him. But how do you know that their disobedience was not part of God's plan? The story of original sin is the story of man's descent into matter, and the question is whether the decision to take this step belonged only to the human beings concerned or whether the Lord had his own marvellously inscrutable, far-reaching plan which allowed human beings a certain freedom of choice, the choice between remaining in paradise or going out to explore the other regions of creation.

The Fall, as it is known in many religions, is simply the choice that the first human beings made to descend into the world of matter in order to find out all about it. The image of a tree also expresses this idea. When Adam and Eve were in paradise they could be said to dwell amongst the flowers in the higher branches of the tree, where all was light, warmth, life, beauty, and freedom. Then they began to wonder about this tree. What exactly was it? Where did the sap come from? What was the source of all that energy? They could see the trunk below them, but there was something else below that. What was it? They wanted to know. And as one can only know things by delving into them and making direct contact, they left the magnificent dwelling in which they were in close touch with heaven and slid down the trunk of the tree into its roots. Then they began to suffer, because, of course, the conditions they found there were very different from those they had been accustomed to, and they felt crushed and stifled by the darkness that weighed on them.

The great consolation in all this is that the life that human beings once knew in paradise is still within us; its imprint can never be erased. From time to time, through beauty, music, or poetry, we hear an echo of that harmony and splendour and taste once again the sweetness of paradise. Paradise exists within the soul of every human being because every human being once dwelt in paradise, but people's lives today are so dreary and banal, and so limited in scope, that there is nothing to remind them of it. Every now and then when they immerse themselves in a mystical text, meet certain people, see a lovely landscape, or listen to a beautiful piece of music, something awakens deep within them; once again they experience a few moments of paradise. Unfortunately, this never lasts more than a few minutes; they soon forget it and sometimes even reject it as an illusion. It is a great pity that people have this attitude, for these heavenly states of consciousness express something real, something that is more real than anything else in fact, and it is highly desirable to live such moments as often as possible until we are at last back in paradise, restored to the bosom of the Lord.

Yes, we shall one day return to paradise; God is still there, waiting to welcome and embrace us. He is not angry with human beings; on the contrary, he is waiting for them and looking forward to the day when they will return to him. But he has given them all eternity in which to make up their minds, for he is very understanding. He says, `They are going to suffer for a while—a few million years perhaps—but afterwards they will come back, and their joy will be so great that they will forget all the rest. Their spirit is immortal; there is no harm in a little suffering. What is a few million years compared to all eternity?' This is how the Lord envisages things. As you see, his reasoning is not ours; he is in less of a hurry than we are.

In the meantime, while they are waiting to return to the embrace of the Lord, human beings are learning a great deal. Now that they have begun to explore matter they are going to have to go all the way. As long as they lived in the divine world there was no need for them to move, but now that they are in the material world they are obliged to follow the experience through all its phases. Suppose you are on top of a mountain: if you are sensible and take care not to slip, you can stay up there as long as you like. But as soon as you set foot on the downward path you are obliged to follow it, slipping and stumbling over boulders and through thorns, in constant danger of falling over the edge of a precipice. Once you set a law or mechanism in motion, the consequences no longer depend on you; you are no longer free to do what you want; you have to run the gauntlet of all the difficulties and dangers inherent in the situation.

You must not imagine that the history of human beings unfolded without God's consent, or that their disobedience and the ups and downs of their destiny were not foreseen. Man chose to turn from God, but God cannot have been absolutely opposed to this decision; otherwise it would quite simply not have been possible. In a sense we can say that everything that man does is done with God's consent. And now man is on his way back to God. After involution comes evolution (reintegration, as it is called in initiatic science), man's reunion with his eternal Father.

You only have to think of the parable of the prodigal son to see that this idea of reintegration is not in contradiction to anything in the philosophy of Jesus. I am sure that you all know this parable. A young man left home and went off to a foreign country where he squandered all his money. After a while he had nothing left and was obliged to take a job herding swine. He was so hungry that he would gladly have eaten the acorns that were fed to the swine, but he was not allowed to. Then he remembered that in his father's house there had always been an abundance of food, and he decided to go home. Jesus summed up the whole history of mankind in this story. And you must remember how the father received his son: recognizing him while he was still far off, he ran to embrace him and ordered his servants to kill the fatted calf and prepare a feast to celebrate his return.

This is exactly what I have been telling you: the Lord is waiting for mankind to return to him after they have finished exploring the world. Human beings were curious about things and wanted to experience them firsthand; why should God stand in their way? He knew in advance that they would be miserable, that they would be hungry and thirsty, that they would suffer, because they would never find anyone to love them as he loved them; but he also knew that in the long run they would come back to him, and everything would be all right again. People always think that God must be angry with men and women because of their sins. Not at all. He lets them do as they please. He has his own plans, and he knows that, sooner or later, his children will return to him. Like the father in the parable of the prodigal son, he is preparing a feast to celebrate their return.

Chapter Two

THE WHEEL OF LIFE

Of all the questions that have preoccupied the minds of men, the most puzzling and the most difficult to answer satisfactorily has always been the reason for the existence of evil. Why does evil exist?

The answer is, in fact, very simple. An illustration will help you to understand. In the old days people often drew water from a well by means of a wheel to which were yoked two teams of oxen, horses, or even men. An observer on the ground would see one team of oxen pulling towards him and the other going away, apparently pulling in the opposite direction. But if this observer had been able to look at the scene from above, it would have been obvious to him that both teams were pulling in the same direction and collaborating in the same task.

This example can help us to understand that good and evil, which seem to be in opposition to each other, are actually two forces harnessed to the same task. It is because we do not look at them from above—that is, from a spiritual, initiatic point of view—that we think they are opposed to each other. If you look at facts and events from below, from the level on which they occur, you will inevitably be mistaken in your judgements. But if you try to move to a higher plane and look at them from the point of view of wisdom, the point of view of the spirit, you will see them as they are. You will see a circle, a wheel, and you will understand that good and evil are two forces that are yoked together to keep the wheel of life turning.

If you annihilated evil, good would also be annihilated. Of course, this does not mean that we should nourish and reinforce evil—it is quite strong enough without any help from us—but neither should we try to eliminate it. In any case, we would not succeed. Rather, we should learn to use it and adopt the right attitude toward it. Yes, the time has come to give mankind a new philosophy.

No doubt, if you dwelt in the sun you would never know obscurity. But you have left the sun, you are living on earth; and as the earth revolves, you are alternately in darkness and in the light. As you are no longer in the sun you have to accept this alternation of night and day, light and darkness, good and evil. And not only accept it, but learn to use it. If darkness is evil, how do you explain the fact that the most significant realizations are conceived in darkness—in the darkness of the earth, or of the subconscious? Darkness is a precondition for all birth or rebirth. Why does a child or a seed begin to grow in darkness? And what about you? How do you use the night? Wonderfully: you spend the night asleep, and when you wake up in the morning, your energy is renewed and you are ready to go back to work.

You ask, 'Yes, but where does evil come from in the first place?' Well, as you know, there is an eternal Principle which is the source of all that exists, and this eternal Principle directed the Elohim to form the earth. Now the Elohim worked with the two principles, masculine and feminine, positive and negative (all manifestation requires the two poles), and inevitably there was a certain amount of material left over, certain elements that were not organized or used and which are not in harmony with the whole. Although these energies and elements are not evil in the eyes of the Creator or the archangels, they are harmful for human beings who have not yet learned to use them.

Let me give you another example. In your

houses there is a place reserved for a rubbish bin and also for a toilet. Whatever your activities, and however enlightened and wise you may be, you will always need to dispose of such things as waste-paper, empty boxes and bottles, fruit peelings or remnants of food, and so on. Your body also needs to get rid of its wastes. You all know this. You all know that there is a negative aspect to even the best things on earth. Yes, everyone knows this, but why is it that they never understand what such details of their everyday lives mean? When the earth was created, all the materials that were left over—bits of brick, broken window-panes, bent nails or twisted planks, symbolically speaking—had to be put somewhere. This is why the earth also has its rubbish-dumps which form a dark cone behind it. This is the earth's shadow (I wonder if astronomers know this).

The source of evil is there, in the remnants left over from the construction of the earth; and as rubbish always attracts animals, ants, flies, maggots, and so on, those who visit these rubbish dumps, expecting to find pleasure and enjoyment, inevitably meet only vermin. This is the region we call hell, the world of darkness, and its function is to be a dumping ground for the rubbish bins of the world. This is where the world's impurities are collected.

Why do certain creatures go to such a region in search of happiness? Because, just as there are human beings in the world who are so poor that they have to hunt for scraps of food or cast-off shoes in other people's rubbish bins, in the psychic world too there are the poor who cannot afford to eat in the restaurants on high, in the company of God and his angels and archangels. They do not have the money (the qualities and virtues) they need to buy the pure, luminous food that comes from the sun, so they are obliged to go and eat the filth that is served in the restaurants frequented by the depraved creatures of hell.

There is great wealth to be found in the unorganized forces and the evil of this region, however, and if you could only learn from the earth how to transform every kind of waste, you would find elements and forces fit to nourish even the angels. Yes, why not? Human beings have already discovered chemical processes by which to purify polluted water. Nature possesses all the means needed to recycle wastes, and human beings have these same means within them; they only need to find them and learn to use them. But before they can do this they are going to have to understand what good is. Only when one understands what good is can one confront evil.

Good is the eternal, creative, all-powerful principle. Good is God himself... and yet in reality God transcends good. The Cabbalah presents good and evil as two manifestations of a higher power. But it is easier to understand if we say that God is the principle of good. Good is a manifestation of God, and evil is a waste-product of good, a remnant that was left over and has never fitted into the harmony of the cosmos. Evil, therefore, can never really be compared to good. It has not received the gift of eternity, nor the power, nor the wealth of good. It would be an error, therefore, to see good and evil as two entities of equal power locked in a constant struggle in which neither can win the ultimate victory.

Evil, as I have said, is a left-over, a residue of good. It is like the pulp that remains after the essence has been extracted from the petals of a rose or other flower. It is matter that has not been refined, and that cannot, therefore, reflect the Deity. Evil is what remains when all the good has been extracted. This means that where there is good there will also necessarily be evil, for evil is the offscourings of good; it has no independent existence. Evil depends on good; it is born of good; it is created by good. As long as human beings think of evil as having its own existence independently from good, they will never be capable of transforming it, and it will continue to torment them. It is they, through ignorance, who give evil this independence and this power over them.

It is light that gives birth to darkness. Where there is light there will inevitably be shadows, for objects cast shadows merely by their presence. Without light there can be no shadows. You may say, 'But perhaps darkness reigns precisely because light is absent.' No, even if an area is in total darkness it is because something is getting in the way of the light. This is why one half of the earth is always in darkness. Without light, darkness could not exist; without good, there would be no evil.

The manifestations of evil are necessary, therefore, but they are neither absolute nor eternal; they are dependent on the forces of good. This means that to solve the problem of evil we have to go beyond good, and before we can go beyond good we have to have a clear idea of what it is. Good is a harmonious manifestation embracing elements of love, strength, intelligence, beauty, gentleness, and so on. As I have already said, good is not God himself. It is a manifestation of God, but it is not God. God transcends both good and evil; we cannot know what he is.

No, we cannot know what God is, but since good is a manifestation of God, of the Creator of the universe, of the eternal Principle, we can be in communion with God by thinking of good. We can lift our consciousness above the dark realms in which all is suffering, anguish, and terror, and unite ourselves with the Centre, with the Author of all that is. And since it is God who created every element, force, and being, he knows exactly what role each is meant to play and how to put things right. Left to ourselves we cannot know, but since God is greater than both good and evil and possesses all powers, it is to him that we should go for help. In this way we shall be capable of setting in motion tremendously subtle forces and putting them to work throughout the universe.

For a disciple, nothing is more worthwhile or more glorious than this work. And there is no need to worry if you do not see tangible results immediately. Most people work on the physical plane and aim only for material success. This is why they are always dissatisfied, for material achievements do not last. Only when you make up your minds to work with the most inaccessible of beings, with God himself, will your achievements be real, for they will be within you, in your own consciousness. And such achievements are instantaneous. That which seems the farthest away is, in fact, the nearest. It is the reality that seems closest that is the farthest away, and try as we might to live in it and make it ours, we can never do so. Only when you begin to work with the most distant realities will you instantly live in them.

Yes, if you want immediate results you must fix your sights on the farthest possible goal. Tell yourself here and now that you have at last understood that truth, power, and life are to be found only in this unique centre which transcends good and evil. Think about this centre, unite yourself with it constantly. Seek nothing else, put your trust in nothing else, work with nothing else. If you ally yourself with this centre it will trigger the forces of good, and they will begin to manifest themselves in an enhancement of your own inner life, and progressively in the world around you.

Why is it so much easier to do evil than good? It is certainly not because good is weak and evil powerful. No, no. It is because human beings have gradually created conditions here on earth that are more conducive to evil. If you are bent on doing evil you will have no difficulty in finding any number of people to give you a helping hand. The situation is quite different when it comes to doing good; it is as though good were paralysed, chloroformed, and impotent. This is always the case in the lower regions of reality, and human beings live too much in those regions. As soon as one manages to get out of these regions, however, the situation is reversed, and it is the turn of evil to be stifled, fettered, and bound. Those who dwell in the higher regions find it impossible to do evil and very easy to do good.

Let me illustrate this. If you tried to set fire to a forest in winter, when everything was wet and covered with snow, you would not succeed; the fire would not take. But in summer, when everything is hot and dry, the merest splinter of glass can focus the sun's rays and very easily start a fire. It is as though the whole forest agreed to burn because conditions were right. Similarly, you cannot fire a cannon if the powder is damp. And so on and so forth. You understand now why evil is so much more powerful than good on earth: human beings have created the most propitious conditions for it. But one day all this will change and the situation will be reversed. Evil will no longer be free to manifest itself; conditions will be against it.

If you want to overcome, control, and transform evil, it is not enough to be a servant of good, because, as I have pointed out, the power of good is limited. The fact that good has never managed to defeat evil means that good is not God himself; it is only one half of God. Evil is the other half. Good and evil are like brother and sister; they are not the father. It is to the father that we must dedicate our lives, for it is he who has authority over his son and daughter (or his two sons, if you prefer). To dedicate one's life to the father is to become the servant of God and not only of good. We have to rise to a higher plane to serve God, who alone has authority over good and evil. Only on this higher plane can we be truly safe. Of course, there is no evil in the higher world, and to the extent to which good means perfection we can say that to be the servant of good is to be the servant of God. But good as it is normally understood intellectually—as the antithesis of evil—is not God. As I say, it is only one half of God.

I could give you many other examples to illustrate the truth of what I have been telling you. Take the way in which the blood circulates in our bodies, for instance. If the blood flowed only in the arteries, life would not be possible, for our organism needs to get rid of its wastes, and this is the function of the veins, the other half of the circulatory system. The veins carry the blood to the lungs where it is purified and sent on to the heart to be pumped back through the arteries. The clean blood—which represents good—flows from the heart therefore. True, but this good is soon charged with impurities and has to be cleansed again... and so it goes on. The same pattern can be seen in the organization of traffic on a highway: the cars going in opposite directions stay on opposite sides of the road. If there were only one-way streets and cars always had to go in the same direction, how would motorists ever get back home?

There is nothing evil in the fact that two forces exist and work in apparently opposite directions, for they can actually be working towards the same end. It is evil only if, instead of collaborating as cosmic intelligence intended, they collide and conflict and neutralize each other. We see this with fire and water. Extraordinary things can be achieved by putting water on a fire. True, but only if there is some kind of barrier between them, for if fire is in direct contact with water, either the water evaporates or the fire is extinguished. This is precisely what happens in every area of life when people are ignorant. Forces and poisons are harmful to human beings only if they are too ignorant and too weak to use them. For nature there is no such thing as evil.

It would even be true to say that evil is contained within good. Take the example of nutrition. We extract from the food we eat only the elements required to keep our bodies healthy, and we eliminate those that cannot be assimilated and would poison us if we could not get rid of them. Evil therefore exists within the good; they are tied to each other, and it is up to our organism to sort them out and eliminate the evil. Or take yet another example. Let's say that a young man falls in love with and marries a charming, ravishingly beautiful girl. This is something good. Yes, but the young man is not alone in admiring his wife's beauty. Others fall under the spell of her charms, and the trouble begins: suspicions, jealousy, quarrels... and sometimes far worse. Or perhaps you have inherited a vast fortune. How wonderful, all of a sudden, to find yourself immensely rich. Yes, but with your fortune come all kinds of cares: people are always asking for money; you are constantly afraid of burglars; you never know a moment's peace. And so it goes in every area of life. Only wisdom is capable of using both good and evil, and, above all, of making sure that good does not become evil.

As I said earlier, good and evil are yoked to the same wheel. If only good existed it could not keep the wheel turning. I may be the only person who dares to say that good is not capable of doing its work without a helping hand from evil. I know that you will object that evil is opposed to good, but that is just the point—it has to be opposed. When you want to cork or uncork a bottle, your two hands collaborate by working in opposite directions: one pushes this way and the other that, and thanks to this opposition you succeed in drawing the cork or in pushing it into the neck of the bottle. Can you at last see how it is possible for opposing forces to work together to achieve a common goal? You have the process before your eyes every day, and yet you cannot see it.

In conclusion, let me tell you that you must remember to link yourself every day to the Lord, to this central point which contains all that is. And it is he, the eternal, indefatigable, indestructible Lord, who never rests and who transcends even good itself, it is he who will call up the forces of good and send them to cleanse and organize everything most marvellously.

Chapter Three

BEYOND GOOD AND EVIL

You could say that there are two schools of thought: the school of good and the school of evil. Adepts of the school of good are advised to reject everything evil in the hope that by so doing they will be saved. Those who follow the teaching of evil combat good in the belief that they can destroy it. But there is another, higher, school of thought which far transcends both these lesser schools, because it knows not only how to use good, it also achieves spectacular results by using homoeopathic doses of evil. This school rejects nothing; it teaches that evil exists only because God allows it to exist. Without this it would have disappeared long ago.

Yes, the fact that evil exists means that God has not vetoed its existence. If this were not so we should have to admit that God had an enemy more powerful than himself, and this, of course, would mean that God was not the all-powerful

Lord of the universe. If a power capable of standing up to God existed in the universe, who could have created it? Another God more powerful than the first? As a matter of fact, human beings have often believed this. They would say, 'What good is God if he is not all-powerful? He does not know everything, he cannot prophecy or work miracles; whereas the devil can do both. We should be much better off with the devil.' In one way you might say that they reasoned correctly. What is to be gained by serving a feeble, incompetent god if all knowledge and all gifts come from his adversary the devil? Even the Church had this attitude: when somebody worked a miracle, the Church declared it to be the work of the devil. There have always been religious leaders who refused to admit that it was God who worked miracles; in their estimation he was incapable of doing so. So it is no wonder that people were ready to sign a pact with Satan. It was the logical solution. Yes, and this is the kind of thing that happens when the so-called spiritual elite have lost the keys to true knowledge.

Perhaps you will ask why, if God is really all-powerful, he does not come and rescue us from all our suffering and distress. The reason is that we have built too many barriers. So many false and arbitrary ideas separate us from God that he cannot reach us to help us. The result is that human beings are convinced that God is too remote and inaccessible to hear their prayers, whereas the devil, who is very close, hears and answers them. Make your own investigation and you will see that this is true. Most people will tell you that although they have prayed to God for a long time, they have never managed to reach him, so they have decided that he must be deaf or asleep. The devil, on the other hand, is always wide awake, and comes as soon as he is called. Well, that is true, but what human beings do not know is that it is they who have distanced themselves from God; it is they who have created the gulf that now separates them from God. In reality no other being is as close to us as God; no other being loves us as much, or is as ready and anxious to help us as God. But we still have to get rid of all that stands in the way of his love and prevents it from reaching us.

Perhaps you remember that I spoke to you one day about the power of the sun, and I said that the sun holds the planets in orbit in the heavens, that it makes trees and plants grow, and causes epidemics, wars, and all kinds of upheavals on earth, simply by changing the currents it emits; and yet this same sun is powerless to enter your house if your curtains are drawn. However many hours you spend entreating the sun to come in and fill your house with its beautiful light, if your curtains are closed it will be unable to do so. It will tell you, 'I cannot get in—you must draw back your curtains.' We behave as though we expected God to draw our curtains for us. But he will not do it. In fact, at the risk of seeming sacrilegious, I tell you that the all-powerful God is powerless to reach you if your curtains are closed. It is you who have to throw them open.

In any case, you must not think that the reason why God has allowed evil to manifest itself in the world is that he is incapable of defeating it. Above all, you must not believe—as many Christians believe—that he needs the help of human beings to get rid of it. Imagine how helpful they would be. No, you will perhaps be surprised, but I have to tell you that evil is necessary—indispensable in fact—to the work of nature, for nature knows how to make use of it. Nature uses evil just as pharmacologists use certain poisons to manufacture very potent medicines. Evil is a poison which can be deadly for the weak and ignorant, but which can be a panacea, a remedy, for those who are strong and intelligent. This is what the third school teaches: how to use evil.

The world is full of clues that are intended to enlighten human beings and get them to reflect on these things, about how to use their trials and difficulties. Why do people never learn this? It is a problem that every disciple should work at. Suppose you see someone coming towards you and you think that he is an enemy, so, without giving him a chance to show that he is actually a friend, you attack and kill him. Tragedies of this kind sometimes happen. You must learn to study the 'enemy' who is bothering you, and perhaps you will find that he is not as hostile and dangerous as you thought. You may even find that he can become your friend.

We experience the forces of evil as being hostile, but in fact they have no hostility towards us. It is simply that everything that does not exactly suit us seems hostile. This is only normal: elements that poison or paralyse us are seen as hostile; everything that vibrates on a different wavelength or puts obstacles in our way, everything that obscures or perturbs our consciousness, is our enemy. But does this state of affairs have to last for ever? No; for if you manage to transform these forces and elements they will be beneficial to you. Let me give you some examples.

A long time ago, fire, lightning, water, and wind were enemies, and human beings battled against them and many died in the battle. But once they learned to domesticate these forces they understood that they had been their enemies only because they had not known how to domesticate them and make them work for them. Why should we not do exactly the same with other forces that we encounter in life? The truth is that evil represents very potent forces to which we cannot relate well, simply because we do not know how to harness and use them. And, of course, when one does not know how to use something there is always a chance of being hurt by it. The case of electricity is one of the most striking examples of what human beings can do to channel a force that would destroy them instantly if they tried to handle it in its raw state. Look at all those wires, transformers, appliances and switches... Mankind has succeeded in taming electricity so completely that today even a baby can use it without danger.

So there you are, it is all very clear and easy to understand: when we look more closely at forces that we are accustomed to think of as evil we discover that they are not evil at all, for there is no such thing as evil in nature.

The earth is far more intelligent than human beings. We give it all our filth and wastes, and it accepts them as something very precious and transforms them into plants and flowers and fruit. And what about coal? How was it formed? And oil? And precious stones? The wisdom that makes this possible exists therefore, and since the earth and certain initiates possess it, since God possesses it, why should we not try to possess it also? For thousands of years human beings have been imploring God to destroy evil, but God only scratches his head and smiles, saying, 'Poor little things. When they understand that they need evil they will stop asking me to get rid of it.' But until this realization dawns, the prayers will continue. We have to pray, to be sure, but for something quite different. We should say, 'Lord, show me your design for the world. Let me see how you envisage things. Grant me wisdom, understanding, and intelligence, so that, like you, I can put myself beyond the reach of evil. Teach me how to use evil, how to accomplish great things with it.' There are so many things in life that show us that what is evil for some is not necessarily evil for others. Some animals can stand extremes of heat, others of cold; some can neutralize poisons, others can go for long periods without food. Some even survive when they are cut in two. Human beings have forged their own notions of evil, and these notions are not universally applicable. This is what I am trying to get you to understand: we have our ideas, our conception of evil, but there are other creatures in the universe who, having reached a higher degree of evolution and learned how to use evil, understand it differently.

A few more examples will make this even

clearer. If you fill your stomach with water there will be no harm done, but if you fill your lungs with water you will be in trouble. To fill your lungs with air is good, but to fill your stomach with air is much less good. From this we can conclude that something may be good in one place but evil in another. If your eyes are sore, for instance, light can hurt them. This means that even light can be good or bad depending on the persons concerned. It also means that human beings will never know what evil is as long as they can only judge it in relation to their own faults and failings. When they begin to be more nearly perfect their opinion will change. This is why the view of the man in the street is so different from that of sages and initiates. An initiate sees beyond what terrifies the weak and finds in evil a benevolent force, a friend and ally.

In any case, the best way to weaken one's resistance to evil is to see it as an enemy. When you come up against a difficulty of some kind, you must learn to treat it as a foundation, a good, solid fulcrum on which to base your work. If you have already done some mountaineering you will have learned that it is the snags and rough surfaces of the rock that provide a toe-hold and make it possible to climb up. If you want your life to be smooth and with no rough edges, how will you ever get to the top? Above all, how easy it will be to slide all the way down. Fortunately there are always some rough places; it is thanks to them that you are still alive. You must not ask for a smooth, easy life, without suffering or sorrow, obstacles or enemies, because without them you would have nothing to hold on to and pull yourself up by. If you were given all the things you ask for—money, pleasure, and an easy, untroubled life—there would soon be nothing left of your inner being. It is just as well that heaven turns a deaf ear to your prayers. Everybody begs for a life of ease and opulence without realizing that what they are asking for would be their greatest misfortune.

I know that it is difficult to accept what I am saying. Every day I give you a different aspect of this philosophy, and sometimes you are upset by my ideas because they do not correspond to yours. But I want you to get rid of your ideas and try mine for a change. You will see what a difference they make. But you refuse. You insist that you want power, money, and glory; you want the whole world to admire you. Heavens, what strange things human beings want. One wants a business with multiple branches; another wants to own a night club or a beauty salon. As for the women and girls who long to be film stars or beauty queens... they dream of all the men who would accost them as they walk their lap dogs, for they know very well that when a man exclaims, 'Oh what a cute little dog. What a beauty!' what they are really interested in is the dog's mistress… and they are secretly hoping to make her their own. If we could see what was in the hearts of men and women we would have to laugh... or perhaps to cry.

Since evil represents forces and materials so explosively powerful that we have not yet gained control over them, we should remind ourselves that we still have the possibility of reaching a higher level and acquiring this control. As long as something is beyond our control it can be evil for us. It is up to us, therefore, to become more perfect and reach a level that is above evil, where we shall be in a position to transform it into good. How do you feed an infant? If you gave it the food and drink of an adult you could kill it, but when it grows up and becomes stronger, that same food and drink will no longer harm it. As you see, our daily lives are full of such examples. You have all noticed them, but you have not drawn the right conclusions from them. You must get into the habit of observing the facts of life.

The reason why human beings have such mistaken ideas about good and evil is that they have side-stepped the true problem; they do not know that what is evil for some can be good for others. But when disciples learn to strengthen themselves and reach a deeper, truer understanding of things, the evil that cripples, poisons, or annihilates others will only make them more beautiful, nobler, and healthier. What do we do to protect ourselves from rain or snow or tornadoes? Do we go out and shout at the forces of nature to calm down? Well, this may be what people in fairy-tales do, but in the ordinary way of life we take care of our houses and make sure that they are sturdy and well insulated, and that the heating system is adequate. Yes, you know well enough what to do on the material plane, but when it comes to your inner life you behave like ignoramuses and try to do away with evil. Why do you continue to struggle against evil instead of concentrating on becoming stronger and making an effort to understand better and act accordingly?

Of course, if you are already seriously ill, it is not easy to fortify yourself sufficiently to overcome your illness. But that is because for years and years—for countless incarnations, in fact—you have done everything possible to make yourself ill, and now you are going to have to work for the same length of time to restore your health. This does not contradict what I have just been saying. You have done everything possible to make yourself weak, anaemic, ignorant, and benighted, and you have succeeded. We cannot deny that evil exists, but we must understand that it is we ourselves who have nurtured it, and if we change our understanding of it, we can either weaken and dispel it or make use of it.

I have never denied that the majority of human beings live in difficult and sometimes catastrophic conditions. You would have to be blind to fail to see the sad, pitiable, deplorable reality. But I still insist that you should be happy. Sometimes I sense that you have a movement of inner revolt. You think, 'The Master does not see the appalling conditions we have to put up with.' Oh, but I do see, I see them all around us. But I also see something else. I can see the good conditions which are also very real, but which you cannot see because your difficulties absorb all your attention. What I see most clearly are the good conditions, the great wealth and all the treasures that exist within you, whereas you see only your external conditions. When you begin to understand me you will feel stronger and will realize that you needed to be encouraged by someone who sees the positive side of things. Yes, you look only at your weaknesses and your poverty, or the fact that your wife has left you, or your children refuse to listen to reason. But there are so many other things to see.

While you are listening to me, of course, you

feel full of courage, but in an hour's time you will have forgotten all your courage and inspiration. The first little difficulty you encounter—a sour look or a cross word—deflates you. I have seen this so often: the slightest blow bowls you over.

The great thing to remember is that what is evil for some can be good for others. If you hold on to this idea it will be a tremendous help. Once you understand that evil is not absolute—that it is relative in fact—it will be much easier for you to put up with it, and you will see that you begin to be unaffected by things that used to make you suffer. You will even feel that heaven has set you free. This has been the experience of so many initiates: they came to realize that all that they had lost and all the trials they had endured had simply been the means of their liberation. You too must adopt this philosophy; otherwise, when you should be singing canticles of praise and thanksgiving to the Lord, you will always find some excuse to be miserable. From one day to the next, through the light of understanding, evil can be transformed into good; whereas if you fail to understand and fail to use it, it will always be evil.

There you are then—a bright future awaits you. The possibilities these truths give you are fantastic. If you have really understood, nothing will hold you back. Since human beings have succeeded in using the forces of nature—winds, waterfalls, and tides—they are certainly capable of the same success on the psychic plane; it is simply a question of attitude. The one thing that is essential is to understand that you must not struggle against evil.

There have been occultists who died because they declared war on evil and attacked it head-on. Being ignorant of these truths, they ventured out alone to do battle with evil; it was inevitable that they would be reduced to dust. I am not saying that initiates must not combat evil, but before doing so they must prepare and purify themselves for a long time so that the Lord may enter and dwell within them and manifest his omnipotence through them. Only God himself can annihilate evil. We have neither the height, nor the breadth, nor the power, nor even the methods that would enable us to do so. Read the Apocalypse, the Book of Revelation, and you will see that the Archangel Mikhaël will bind the Dragon, symbol of all evil, and shut him up for a thousand years. Think what this means: if even this all-powerful archangel is not going to destroy evil but only shut it up, how can we, poor miserable creatures that we are, hope to do away with it?

Many of you will certainly be surprised by this new conception of evil. But it is simply the conclusion I have drawn from my own observations, and there is nothing to prevent you from making your own observations of the same things every day. The trouble is that human beings are not in the habit of reflecting on the minor events of their daily lives, in order to understand and interpret what they tell us. And yet it is there, in our own lives and in nature, that the most important philosophical problems are exposed and resolved—and with far greater ease and clarity than in any tomes of abstract philosophy.

Evil, as we have seen, is a force that is still chaotic, and it torments human beings because they are not yet capable of controlling or using it. But when a disciple begins to see how he can use what he has always thought of as evil in order to make greater progress in his spiritual life, he gradually gains control of his situation. As it is impossible to conquer evil, we must replace such words as 'fight', 'kill', 'uproot', and 'exterminate' (which express a false notion of evil) by such words as 'tame', 'assimilate', 'channel', 'orientate', 'sublimate', and 'use' (which express a more advanced and more spiritual notion). In this way the opaque blackness of coal becomes a bright, luminous red. Is the problem one of sexual energy, anger, jealousy, or a desire for revenge? Is it an adversary, an illness or a temptation of some kind? Whatever the problem, this new philosophy gives us the conditions that are most conducive to working, becoming stronger, and finding lasting solutions to all our problems.

And now one last word of advice: whenever you are tempted to think that something that befalls you is evil, ask yourself whether it really is bad, or whether it is not, rather, a blessing in disguise. If you never ask yourself this question you will either try to eliminate whatever it is that is bothering you, or you will waste your energy in helpless fury. In either case you will get no benefit from it, simply because you fail to see the hidden good. Human beings are rarely capable of recognizing whether something is good or bad for them. Sometimes they are so used to certain situations that they are convinced they are good for them, while in fact they are very dangerous. Think of all those who have been destroyed by success. And think also of those who have been capable of using every obstacle or failure as a springboard from which to leap to ultimate triumph. But one has to live for a very long time, study deeply, and endure many trials and ordeals before being capable of seeing how true this is.

Chapter Four

THE WHEAT AND THE WEEDS

The Kingdom of heaven may be compared to someone who sowed good seed in his field; but while everybody was asleep, an enemy came and sowed weeds among the wheat and then went away. So when the plants came up and bore grain, then the weeds appeared as well. And the slaves of the householder came and said to him, 'Master, did you not sow good seed in your field? Where, then, did these weeds come from?' He answered, 'An enemy has done this.' The slaves said to him, 'Then do you want us to go and gather them?' But he replied, 'No, for in gathering the weeds you would uproot the wheat along with them. Let both of them grow together until the harvest; and at harvest time I will tell the reapers, Collect the weeds first and bind them in bundles to be burned, but gather the wheat into my barn.

Matthew 13, 24-30

Jesus often illustrated his teaching with images taken from the life of farmers—fields, seeds, and so on—and as he interpreted them for us himself, there is no need for me to do so. There is just one thing I want to talk about today, and that is the landowner's response to his servants when they asked if they should uproot the weeds: 'No, for in gathering the weeds you would uproot the wheat along with them. Let both of them grow together until the harvest.'

When you understand this parable you will have understood one of the most important laws of life: how to grow and advance in spite of the seemingly adverse conditions that destiny allots to you; how to behave according to the rules prescribed by this landowner: 'Let the wheat and the weeds grow together until the harvest.'

From both the educational and the social point of view, this is an extremely important rule of conduct. People are forever crying out against the wicked, demanding that they be killed and exterminated, but since the world began it has never been possible to do away with all the wicked. Even today educators, religious teachers, and moralists still tell us to uproot our vices and bad habits. No doubt the intention behind this advice is excellent, but how can it be put into effect? They all brandish weapons with which they say they are going to annihilate evil, and yet it has never ceased to exist. Sometimes, in fact, when one succeeds in uprooting one minor vice one becomes a prey to others that are far worse.

People try to eliminate evil in the same way as they try to eliminate mosquitoes: they forget to drain the swamps in which they breed. You cannot do away with evil by killing off the wicked, because the wicked breed in certain conditions. You have to drain the swamps—that is to say, change conditions—and then there will be no more mosquitoes. You will tell me that you know all this. I do not doubt that for a minute, but what you do not know is that even within you there are swamps in which evil breeds and wicked beings proliferate. You spend your time swatting the mosquitoes that bother you, but you make no effort to drain the breeding ground within you. This is one of those truths that are not very palatable, but it has to be said!

One way of interpreting the parable of the weeds is to say that the field represents the world, and the wheat and weeds represent good men and bad, who will one day be sifted and separated. This interpretation is correct, but it is incomplete. The wheat-field represents the world, true, but it also represents each human being, for within each human being are both wheat and weeds—that is, both a good and an evil nature.

Of course, you may wonder how it is that

human beings, who were created in the image of God and who have been endowed by God with such magnificent qualities, should manifest so many bizarre tendencies and desires. Why do so many people want to lie and steal and kill and betray each other? How can God create evil, vicious criminals? The parable answers this question: an enemy came while we were asleep and sowed a different kind of seed within us, and now both kinds grow in us together. The words 'while everybody was asleep' explain it all, and this 'sleep' is something that can happen even to the most highly evolved beings. When our consciousness falls asleep, our intelligence is in darkness, and our enemies (that is, a collectivity of many very inferior beings whose goals are contrary to the evolutionary order) sow the seeds of their own perverse thoughts, feelings, and desires in our souls. This is why the disciples of an initiatic school must always be very vigilant, very wide awake, even when they are sleeping. The body may sleep, but never the soul.

Weeds have always been an object of study ever since the world began. In hospitals, schools, and courts of law people continually try to analyse the elements that go to make up weeds. But not only is it impossible to understand evil in all its manifestations, it is also very dangerous to try to uproot it, for it is so inextricably interwoven with good that in trying to uproot the one there is a serious risk that you will also uproot the other. Hermes Trismegistus said that we should: 'Separate the subtle from the gross with great diligence.' Yes, but human beings do not yet have the skill that such an operation requires. The best solution, therefore, is to allow good and evil to co-exist, and learn to use the activity and the extraordinarily potent forces contained in the elements of evil. In other words, human beings must learn to use minute doses of evil to reinforce and enhance the forces of good. The principle is exactly the same as that applied in grafting: a nurseryman takes a cutting from a pear tree that produces big, juicy fruit and grafts it to the stem of a wild tree that produces only small, hard, inedible fruit. In this way the graft benefits from the strength and energy of the wild stock. In the same way we can graft branches of the tree of good on to the tree of evil. Just as evil is allowed to use good as a source of energy, which it then transforms and uses for diabolical ends, good also has the right to draw on the energy of evil, so as to transform and use it for its own ends.

Let me give you an example of how we can do this. We all have organs, whose functions seem to us to be neither spiritual, nor aesthetic, nor particularly clean, but as they are necessary we cannot just get rid of them. Everything in nature is connected to something else. Every cell, every organ is connected to other cells and other organs, just as the roots of a tree are connected to its branches, leaves, flowers, and fruit. If man were to cut off his roots—that is, if he were to get rid of the organs on which his very existence depends—the results could only be disastrous. It is true that these organs are sometimes the cause of tragedies, but we have to allow them to go on living, and try to transform the energies we draw from them.

When one reads the biographies of the great men and women of history it is sometimes very surprising to see how many of them had to contend with abnormal, perverse—even criminal—tendencies. We cannot understand this if we do not understand the structure of human beings. The explanation, in fact, is very simple: it is precisely because they were constantly struggling to overcome these ignoble tendencies that such people achieved greatness. Whether they knew it or not, they were applying the principle of the graft. The succulence of their fruits—the excellence of their achievements—were in direct proportion to the violence and ardour of their passions—that is, to the vigour of their roots. Others, who never have to contend with such defects, live mediocre, insignificant lives and contribute nothing to mankind.

Now I am not suggesting that we should tolerate, excuse, or cultivate the evil that exists in the world. No, but the time has come for human beings to understand this sublime philosophy, and learn how to use the forces of evil for the greater glory of good. The taller the trunk of a tree and the wider the spread of its branches, the deeper must be its roots. Those who do not understand this are horrified to see the dimensions of evil. But there is no need to be afraid; everything in nature is built on laws that are extraordinarily wise. If our roots do not go very deep we shall be incapable of drawing life from the soil, or of resisting gales and tempests.

What should be our attitude towards those who represent the weeds in society? On the surface of the earth there are mountains and plains, and between them flow currents which generate certain manifestations of life. If the earth were completely flat and smooth there would be no life. Jesus never hesitated to make friends with the poor or with sinners and criminals, because he was well aware of this law. Whereas the Pharisees and Sadducees, who were ignorant of the laws of nature, despised Jesus and reproached him for frequenting the ignorant, sinful masses. Their pride created a gulf between them and the poor and disinherited, but Jesus preferred to live with those who were sick and defenceless, with society's rejects, so that there might be some exchange between them. He gave them his light, his love, and his purity, while drawing raw, unrefined energies from them, just as the roots of a tree draw from the soil the raw elements it uses to produce flowers and fruit. The wicked supply the energy, and the good absorb and transform it and distribute it in the form of kindness, charity and wisdom. This exchange is vital. Jesus took upon himself the sins of mankind; in other words, he drew from them raw energies, which he then transformed in the leaves of his being, and gave back to the world in the form of light and love.

Those who refuse all contact with evil and ignorant men, who associate only with the refined, well-read, and virtuous few, will not evolve to any great extent, for they are not good alchemists. They are depriving themselves of the qualities and virtues they need in order to evolve. In spite of all their learning, therefore, the Pharisees were very ignorant, for they held themselves aloof from the masses—although this did not prevent many of them from being even more sinful and vicious than those they despised. Jesus, on the other hand, wanted to plunge into the very dregs of society. He associated with the lowest of the low deliberately, so that he could work to purify them and raise them up to God. The distrust and pride of the Pharisees laid their souls wide open to impurity and weakness, whereas the audacity, confidence, and love of Jesus purified the very atmosphere around him.

I am not telling you this in order to encourage you to frequent degenerates and gaolbirds. Before you do any such thing it is essential to study the question of the wheat and weeds very carefully; in other words, you must begin by learning how to perform the operation I have been talking about, the transmutation of evil into good. I have sometimes seen charming, virtuous women who married drunkards and scoundrels in the hope of saving them; but as good intentions are not enough to drag someone from the clutches of vice, instead of saving their husbands they ended up in the same state of depravity and shame. You cannot transform evil if you do not possess a special kind of knowledge. Initiates are able to help us because they assume the burden of our sins, errors, and weaknesses, and in exchange they give us their light, love, and peace. Only the truly great initiates know how to transmute evil into good, for only they know the properties of the weeds and are capable of using them.

The first thing one notices in this figure is that it represents different categories of human beings that correspond to the different levels of being: physical, astral, mental, causal, buddhic and atmic.

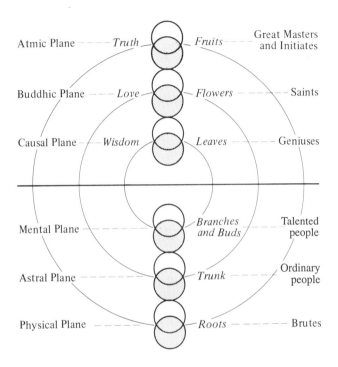

And now let us see how these different human types correspond to the different parts of a tree. The brutes belong in the roots of life; their work is underground. Ordinary men and women work in the trunk, passing the raw materials from below up to a higher plane, where they will be developed and transmuted by others. The talented represent the branches which convey the raw sap to the leaves and then carry the transformed sap back to the roots. The role of the branches is to take, in order to give, to ensure an exchange. Geniuses are the leaf-buds, and it is here that the alchemical process begins and the raw sap is transmuted through the action of the sun's rays. Saints are the flowers of the cosmic tree; butterflies, birds, insects, and human beings are attracted by their beauty, colour, and perfume. Their role is to form the fruits, and it is thanks to them that life becomes pure and beautiful. The great masters are the fruits of the cosmic tree, the celestial manna, the bread from heaven. In them is the sweetness of every quintessence.

Every human being represents a tree, with its roots, trunk, branches, leaves, flowers, and fruit. They all have roots, a trunk, and branches, but as most of them never experience the coming of spring, very few have fruit or flowers, or even leaves; they are like the forlorn, naked trees of winter. Of course, all human beings are potentially capable of flowering, but a great deal of hard work and knowledge, and the sacrifice of much time is needed for their flowers to bloom, to exhale their perfume, and to form fruit. The fruits of a human tree are the work of the different virtues.

Leaves, flowers, and fruit correspond to wisdom, love, and truth. With great wisdom the leaves transform the raw sap into sugar sap, just as alchemists transformed base metals into gold, thanks to the Philosophers' Stone. The flowers have a special rapport with love: all creatures are attracted to them because of their colour and perfume and the purity of their petals. It is in the flowers that insects find the nectar they seek. The fruits of a tree represent truth, for truth is born of the union of wisdom and love.

There comes a season when leaves, flowers, and fruit fall from the tree and only the branches, trunk, and roots are left. And just as the branches, trunk, and roots of a tree are always there, so also are there always plenty of brutes, ordinary men and women, and people of talent in the world; whereas geniuses, saints, and great masters are few and far between. In winter, when the foliage, flowers, and fruits of summer have gone, the beauty of their colour, scent, and flavour remains engraved in our memory. In the same way, for a long time after geniuses, saints, and great masters have left the world, people still speak of their deeds and of the joy they communicated to those around them. Conditions on earth are not conducive to the permanent presence of love, wisdom, beauty and truth. Geniuses, saints and spiritual masters bless the earth with their presence only briefly, whereas ordinary men and women—who represent mediocrity and ugliness—are always present. In heaven, on the other hand, leaves, flowers, and fruit are always present. All the rest is transitory.

Roots, trunk, and branches, which correspond in man to the physical, astral, and mental bodies, represent our lower nature, the personality; leaves, flowers, and fruit, which correspond to our causal, buddhic, and atmic bodies, represent our higher nature, the individuality. If you are observant you will see for yourselves that it is your instincts, passions and personal tendencies—in other words, your roots, trunk and branches—that are the toughest and most stable and tenacious elements in your make-up. From time to time your tree bears a few leaves (luminous thoughts in your intelligence), a few flowers (warm feelings in your soul), and a few meagre fruits (altruistic, unselfish actions). Unfortunately, the season of spring is all too brief! The inspirations and subtle states of consciousness fade very quickly, and you find yourself once again with the same old needs: to eat and drink and quarrel and turn everything to your own advantage.

Now, look at this figure again and you will find even more of these marvellous correspondences in nature. As you can see, it shows that the roots are linked to the fruit. The roots are the point of departure; the fruit is the point of arrival. Once the fruit is ripe, the roots rest from their work. But the extraordinary thing is that the fruit and the seed it bears are the roots of the future from which a new stem will grow. The fact that the fruit of some plants (tubers) grows on their roots is an indication of this bond between roots and fruit. Tubers are plants that have not managed to develop in the spiritual world; they have remained underground.

This figure also indicates a link between the trunk and the flowers, and between the branches and the leaves. And this too can be seen in man, in whom the physical body is linked to the spirit, the heart to the soul, and the intellect to the causal body. This explains the close relationship that exists between brutes and the great masters, between ordinary human beings and the saints, and between men and women of talent and geniuses.

It is not up to us to destroy the wicked; justice belongs to God alone. Our task is to concentrate on good, on studying and working for good. The more we contribute to the spiritual power of good, the more this power will curb the work of the wicked. We must leave it to higher forces to transform the wicked, for we are incapable of doing so. In fact, human beings are deluding themselves when they think that they can rid the world of criminals by executing them, for once they are dead they move to the astral and lower mental planes and become capable of even greater evil. Their thirst for revenge urges them to worm their way into the minds of the living and influence them to commit their crimes for them. They have even more scope for their evil designs than when they were alive, for they are no longer confined to the limits of their own physical body; they can influence the thoughts and feelings of any number of people and use them as their agents.

As long as a foul-smelling liquid is corked up in a bottle the stench cannot spread, but once the bottle is opened the stench spreads and poisons the atmosphere. Similarly, as long as criminals are alive they are confined to their physical body, but as soon as they die their spirit is free to travel far and wide and influence the minds of a great many people. In view of the consequences on the invisible plane, therefore, criminals should not be executed. It is up to us to organize the conditions of life so that there will be no more criminals. A society that is not founded on spiritual principles is like a swamp, and a swamp can only produce mosquitoes.

To conclude, let us listen again to the words of the landowner in the parable: 'At the time of harvest I will say to the reapers, "Collect the weeds first and bind them in bundles to be burned".' The weeds must be thrown into the fire, because only fire has the power to separate good from evil. What is happening when you run a fever? Harvest time is here, perhaps, and you are undergoing a minor harvest—the major harvest would be much harder to bear, and who knows whether, when it is over, you would find yourself safely in the barn or in the fire. When the fever (fire) is on you it melts and consumes your inner weeds. In other words, it rids your system of all its negative, poisonous wastes, and when its work is done, you give a sigh of relief because you feel so much better. There are major and minor harvests, therefore, and the function of a fever is to rid you of certain weeds, for weeds exist on the three planes: physical, astral and mental.

A time will come—indeed it is near—when evil will be driven from the earth. The Archangel Mikhaël will bind the dragon and shut it up for a thousand years. This will be the time of the harvest. The invisible world will send fire to purify the earth, and only then will the wheat within us be set apart from the weeds. Even now the earth is entering the fire, and those whose inner fields are full of weeds will suffer greatly, for the fire that is coming will reach into their innermost being. But those whose fields bear a rich crop of wheat will rejoice. They will be like lamps, and their flames will burn brighter and

brighter, for the fire from heaven which consumes
the weeds will illuminate the sons and daughters
of God.

Chapter Five

THE PHILOSOPHY OF UNITY

I realize that what I have been telling you about evil probably upsets and revolutionizes all your former ideas on the subject. But it will not be very long before the whole world acknowledges the truth of what I say, for this is the only true philosophy, the only one that sees exactly where each element fits into the whole. A time is coming when human beings will no longer be torn by inner conflict, when all contradictions will be replaced by unity. Good and evil will walk hand in hand in the same direction, united in the service of heaven. As long as people continue to see good and evil as mutually contradictory they will continue to tear themselves apart and destroy themselves. What can one do if one is perpetually at war with oneself? This outworn philosophy will never produce peace. Peace and harmony will come only when there is unity, when everything is moving in the same direction.

Look at the human body: the upper part—the mouth, nose, eyes, and brain, for instance—moves us to admiration, but the lower part—the stomach and intestines, and so on—is far less attractive. And yet the upper and lower parts of our bodies work together in close collaboration, and both are indispensable. The fact that human beings always take both parts with them wherever they go is surely proof of this. You will never see people who leave one part of themselves at home while they take only the more presentable and aesthetic part with them when they go out. Why then do they separate the two parts in their minds? Both parts work together to maintain and develop the faculties of the whole person, and if they oppose and combat each other, it means that through ignorance human beings have allowed disorder and divisiveness to take over. In reality, the two aspects are designed to exist and work hand in hand.

Perhaps you will be horrified if I tell you just how far my reflections on the subject have gone. Suppose I asked some ordinary Christians or even some of their puritanical theologians to explain their conception of the kingdom of heaven: 'Tell me, what happens to people when they get to heaven? Are they whole or have they left half of themselves behind? What have they done with the organs that you consider so disgusting and shameful?' The answer would probably be that they had never thought about it. But then their conception of things is incomplete, for they cannot explain how people are constituted when they are in heaven. Do they keep all their organs or only the head, the brain, and the eyes? This is a very awkward question. And it may come as a surprise to you too, because you have probably never thought about it either. Perhaps you will say, 'True, I believe that heaven exists, but what is it like? And where is it? And what are people like when they are in heaven?' I assure you that if heaven were really as many religious people say it is, it would be a very dull place indeed. No wonder they are in such a hurry to come back and reincarnate on earth. No, but joking apart, I am trying to show you that many of the things we believe are neither clear nor logical. If I poke fun at these notions it is because I want you to become aware of certain problems that you had never thought about before. That is my role.

Now you will no doubt be wondering how you will live when you get to heaven. Well, the one thing I know for sure is that God did not create human beings in order to cut them in two. How unsightly that would be; no painter or sculptor could help being disgusted at the sight of such mangled and mutilated human beings. Besides, who would stand to gain from such a

thing? God loves beauty more than anyone, and
he did not create human beings carelessly. No one
even knows how long it took to create them. You
will say that, on the contrary, you do know: it
took just one day, the sixth day of creation. How
well-informed you are! One day. Do you really
believe that it took only one day to create human
beings, with all the gifts and qualities that we can
see, and all those that are still invisible to us, all
their subtle bodies? Try to see the splendour of all
this, and then you will understand why God has
no desire to mutilate human beings by cutting
them in two to please the ignorant.

Duality is simply an expression of unity. One
is the first and only number. We must understand
that only One exists. What do Two, Three, Four
and all the other numbers represent? They are
simply divisions of One. Arbitrarily we divide
One into Two, Three, Four, Five, or Six and so on,
and each division is presented as a new number,
although it is only a different perception of One, a
fragment of One. What is the Two? The One
polarized. Take a magnet: it is polarized, but not
divided; it is one, and remains one. Two is never
separate from One. Any object, even a human
being, has two ends, two poles, but is still only
one whole. And Three? Well, the two poles
remain linked and act on one another to produce a
being, a force, or an object which is the Three.

But Three is not separate from One, either. Four and Five are also new aspects of One. Individually they do not exist; only the One exists.

It has always been believed that each number was a separate entity that existed on its own, as though the Two, the Three, and so on, were on a par with the One. No, only the One exists. The One is the Father, the prime cause and origin of all that is. Human beings have never understood this. They believe that the One and the Two exist independently of each other—in other words, that God and the devil are equals and have equal power. This is completely false. The devil has no separate existence that would enable him to oppose God. The devil is one aspect of unity. He may be a long way from the centre, but he is always part of the whole. He is never cut off, just as a sewage system is never cut off from the city it serves.

Of course, no one has ever presented the problem of evil in this way before. But you can now see that only one number exists, the number One. All other numbers are no more than different aspects, different divisions of the One, which contains them all. It is impossible for anything to exist outside of and apart from God, the One. This is the true philosophy, the philosophy that was taught in the mysteries and temples of old, but it was not given to the masses. The common run of men were kept amused with `playthings' and allowed to believe whatever they pleased.

The only number we need to know therefore is the One, for all other numbers are contained in it. There is no point in going to look for them elsewhere, for we shall not find them. Those who stop looking for the One, which represents God himself, find the devil and his torments instead. This has always been the case: those who choose the Two forget about the One. At certain periods in the history of Christianity, there were so many sculptures and paintings representing the devil and the torments of the damned that people forgot about God. The Good Lord seemed to be powerless compared to the devil. What an aberration. What a regression. The greatest mistake human beings can make is to turn their backs on the One, for when we remain attached to the One, all that is negative and hostile disappears... and that includes the devil himself. Only God remains.

A human being also must be studied from the point of view of unity. Even if he is divided in two—body and soul, individuality and personality, interior and exterior, higher and lower, spirit and matter, emissive and receptive, concave and convex, man and woman, good and evil, heaven and hell—a human being is still one.

He can also be divided in three—head, trunk, and limbs, or head, lungs, and belly—but he is still one. Alchemists divide man being into four; Theosophists into seven; others into nine or twelve. Who is right? They are all right. But however many parts you divide man into he is still one.

Work with the One therefore, for there is neither Two nor Three. Even if you split man up into as many parts as he has organs, nerves, capillaries, cells, and atoms, you will still be dealing with a single being, a unit. It is the unit that matters therefore. To divide man is to mangle, mutilate and destroy him, whereas to consider him as a unit is to preserve his life and vigour.

The One is harmony, fulfilment, immortality; all other numbers bring disintegration. The Two is war, antagonism, good and evil, Ormuzd and Ahriman, day and night. The Three makes peace between them, but only temporarily. Three is the son who embraces his parents and begs them to stop fighting. And for his sake they call a truce, but they still go on arguing, even with their child—you all know how it goes in a family. Then a daughter arrives, making Four, and the endless hostilities begin all over again, because the mother prefers the son and the father prefers the daughter.

Peace is to be found only in the One. This is why you must learn to go beyond both good and evil. Good is not enough, for it has never managed to solve the problem of evil. Although good has always been at war with evil, it has never managed to defeat it. And evil never succeeds in overcoming good. However much evil burns, persecutes, or massacres good, it keeps springing up anew, it keeps growing and spreading, for it too is tenacious. It is no use trying to do anything about good and evil; the only solution is to go over their heads.

In ancient times the philosophy of the initiates was the philosophy of unity. Duality appeared only later, in the Persian religion of Manichaeism, for instance, or in certain forms of Christianity which saw the devil as God's adversary. No, God has no adversaries. He cannot have. All beings defer to God; all creatures obey him, for he is the Creator. We human beings may have adversaries, of course, but that is because we are ignorant and keep breaking the laws, but God cannot have adversaries.

Over and above duality and polarity is the One. I have never said that you should not study the other numbers. On the contrary, you must study them, but without forgetting that they are only aspects, manifestations of the One, to which you must continually return. It is difficult for you to understand me today, but one day you will understand. For the time being, bear in mind that the other numbers exist as separate entities only for purposes of analysis or classification, but in reality the One includes them all.

Chapter Six

THE THREE TEMPTATIONS

Then Jesus was led up by the Spirit into the wilderness to be tempted by the devil. He fasted forty days and forty nights, and afterwards he was famished. The tempter came and said to him, "If you are the Son of God, command these stones to become loaves of bread." But he answered, "It is written, 'One does not live by bread alone, but by every word that comes from the mouth of God.'"

Then the devil took him to the holy city and placed him on the pinnacle of the temple, saying to him, "If you are the Son of God, throw yourself down; for it is written, 'He shall give his angels concerning you,' and 'On their hands they will bear you up, so that you will not dash your foot against a stone.'" Jesus said to him, "Again it is written, 'Do not put the Lord your God to the test.'"

Again, the devil took him to a very high mountain and showed him all the kingdoms of the world and their splendour; and said to him, "All these I will give you, if you will fall down and worship me." Jesus said to him, "Away with you Satan! for it is written, 'Worship the Lord your God, and serve only him.'"

Then the devil left him, and suddenly angels came and waited on him.

Matthew 4, 1-11

'Then Jesus was led up by the Spirit into the wilderness to be tempted by the devil.' This phrase calls for some interpretation, for if it was the Spirit—the Spirit of good—that led Jesus into the wilderness to be tempted, it proves that the spirits that we call evil, because they bring us trials and temptations, are in actual fact servants of God who are carrying out the will of other, more highly evolved entities.

This is by no means the only place in the Bible in which we see the role of the devil. In the Book of Job, for instance, there is an account of a conversation between God and Satan. 'Now there was a day when the sons of God came to present themselves before the Lord, and Satan came also among them.' Satan, as we see, was present at this meeting, and this means that he must have been of some importance, for God does not allow just anyone into such an assembly.

The Lord said to Satan, "Where have you come from?" Satan answered the Lord, "From going to and fro on the earth, and from walking up and down on it." The Lord said to Satan, "Have you considered my servant Job? There is none like him on the earth, a blameless and upright man who fears God and turns away from evil." Then Satan answered the Lord, "Does Job fear God for nothing? Have you not put a fence around him and his house and all that he has, on every side? You have blessed the work of his hands, and his possessions have increased in the land. But stretch out your hand now, and touch all that he has, and he will curse you to your face." The Lord said to Satan, "Very well, all that he has is in your power; only do not stretch out your hand against him!"

Job, 1, 6-12.

This conversation shows clearly that the devil is in the service of God. You are familiar with the rest of the story: how Job was afflicted with every kind of disaster and lost everything he possessed—his flocks, his houses, and even his children—and yet he never cursed the Lord. Later there was another gathering of the sons of God, and the Lord said to Satan, 'You see? You could not make Job curse me.' But Satan replied, 'I did not succeed because he still has his health. But if I rob him of his health he will curse you.' 'Very well,' said the Lord, 'You may take away his health, but you must not take his life.' So Job was afflicted with terrible sufferings. His body was covered with sores and he sat alone on a dunghill, abandoned by all his friends, but he still refused to curse the Lord. In the end God was moved by Job's fidelity and gave him back all the things he had lost—his sons and daughters, his houses and cattle, all his wealth and health—in greater abundance than before, and all those who had derided him became his friends again and acknowledged that he had been right.

At one time the idea of Satan conversing with God shocked some theologians and religious believers so deeply that they said the Book of Job should not be in the Bible at all. It was too contrary to all their conceptions. In point of fact though, this story makes us reflect, and on reflection we find ourselves obliged to acknowledge that it has very profound meaning. It is a gold mine. Goethe used this theme in Faust, which opens with a scene in which God and Mephistopheles are discussing Faust.

It is very interesting to note that when the Lord gave Satan permission to put Job to the test he imposed certain conditions on him. To begin with, he was only allowed to touch Job's possessions, not his person, so Satan robbed Job of his livestock, his servants, and his children. The second time, Satan was allowed to afflict Job's flesh with sores, but not to take his life. And each time, Satan obeyed; he inflicted exactly as much suffering on Job as he was allowed to, and no more; and this shows that those whom we call devils or evil spirits are the servants of God, and that they are doing his will. The entities that come to tempt and test human beings and bring them suffering are simply employees, workers who have been sent to teach them a lesson and advance their evolution.

And now, if we look again at the Gospel text, one very important question arises, for, as we know, Jesus was no ordinary human being. Why did the spirit lead him into the desert to be tempted? This seems to contradict the belief of many Christians who think that Jesus was God himself. If he was God, how could he be tempted? Surely heaven knew him well enough. Are we to think that the heavenly world was not very well informed, and that it needed to test Jesus to know whether he would resist or succumb to temptation?

No, the truth of the matter is that heaven knows all there is to know about us. It knows how much power or patience, endurance or wisdom we have, for it knows exactly what stuff we are made of, just as physicists know the properties of various metals—their weight, density, melting point, and so on. Some metals can be subjected to very high temperatures without melting; others melt more easily. And the same is true of human beings. Each one is made of a specific material, and heaven knows perfectly well whether or not we are going to be able to resist the temptations that come our way. It does not need to put us to the test to find out. It is we who need to find out how strong, faithful, and kind we are or, on the contrary, how weak and vicious we are, so as to realize that we need to work hard to improve ourselves. When we are tested, it is for our own sakes.

In the course of the continual evolutionary process that leads to ever higher levels, human beings need to be tried and tested in order to develop to their fullest capacity. This means that they must first become aware of their inner potential. Just as human beings have to go through certain phases of growth and physical development, when they are sent into this world they also have to pass through certain ordeals, in order to be strengthened spiritually. The only difference between individuals is that each one has to endure trials suited to his or her level of evolution. Some benefit from their trials and others do not. Some people benefit and are enriched by everything; others go under and fail to be transformed. Jesus had to be subjected to the same ordeals that other human beings endure. He may have had nothing more to learn from them, but he had to pass through them.

The nature of the temptations that Jesus was faced with and the reply he gave to each are very significant. This is why it is important to pay close attention to this text, so as to be in a position to adopt the same attitude as Jesus and respond in the same way, for then we too shall triumph over the trials that will inevitably come our way. So, let us take a closer look at the three temptations.

First of all, the devil asked Jesus to change the stones into bread.

Secondly, he asked him to throw himself from the top of the temple, safe in the knowledge that God would send angels to bear him up. Of course, we must see the temple as a symbol; the devil did not carry Jesus physically to the pinnacle of the temple before telling him to throw himself to the ground.

Thirdly, he took Jesus to the top of a mountain and showed him all the kingdoms of the world in all their glory, promising that they would be his if he would only bow down and worship him. The mountain too is symbolic.

These three temptations correspond respectively to the stomach, the heart, and the head—that is to the physical, astral, and mental planes.

In the course of their existence, all human beings have to go through the three phases represented by the stomach, the heart, and the head. As children, they live on the level of the stomach; they are mainly concerned with eating. It is the urge to taste that makes children put everything in their mouths. When they are a little

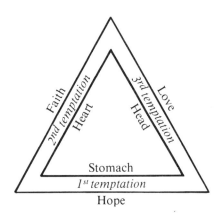

older, it is the heart that manifests itself, and their lives are ruled by love and faith. They feel impelled to abandon themselves to the ardent passions of the heart, trusting that God will send his angels to protect them, and that, even if they fall, the angels will pick them up and wash and care for them. They think that God will make an exception just for them, because they are standing on the pinnacle of the temple of love, veneration, and adoration—adoration of someone who may be quite adorable, no doubt, but who is not necessarily the Creator.

Childhood is linked to the problem of nourishment, and adolescence to that of feelings. But once they are adults, human beings think and reflect. They have more experience, more knowledge, and greater authority. Sensing that they have reached a summit, they tend to become harsh and severe for others; they demand obedience; they are inclined to think that other people should acknowledge their superiority. This is the time of the third temptation which comes from the head, the top of the mountain.

Jesus is not the only one to have been faced with these three temptations. All spiritual masters and all disciples are faced with them. Think of how many occultists are tempted to sell their knowledge, or to use their psychic powers for their own material well-being. Others are so sure of themselves that they are ready to tempt God. In the conviction that, whatever they do, the invisible world will watch over them, they have no hesitation in flinging themselves down from a great height, for they are sure that they will be

protected. But this is false; the invisible world
does not protect the foolhardy. The third
temptation corresponds to yet another phase. A
time comes when a disciple or occultist has
acquired great knowledge. Metaphorically
speaking, he has reached the top of the mountain.
From this vantage point he looks out over the
world and feels capable of dominating it and
claiming its wealth and glory for himself. He
believes himself to be the equal of God.

Now, since we are all obliged to confront
these temptations from the stomach, the heart,
and the head, what should we do in order to be
sure of overcoming them? How should we answer
the spirits—that is, the perverse thoughts and
desires that besiege us? If we look at the way in
which Jesus answered the tempter, we shall see
that he has shown us how to answer according to
the rules of white magic.

To the devil's first suggestion—to change the
stones into bread—Jesus replied, 'It is written,
"One does not live by bread alone, but by every
word that comes from the mouth of God".'
Food—bread—is simply a symbol. Of course,
physical food for the stomach exists, but the air,
perfumes, sounds, light, and colours are also food
for the lungs, the nose, the ears, and the eyes.
They are food of a subtler kind than the physical
food we eat, but you must realize that there are

creatures who are nourished by sounds, perfumes, and colours.

As a rule, people imagine that nothing exists other than minerals, vegetables, animals, and human beings. They have no inkling of the existence of invisible regions inhabited by creatures who are utterly different from themselves and from anything they have ever known. In reality, the whole universe is full of wonderful, extraordinary creatures, and some very advanced human beings have been able to see them and get to know them. You will say that it is very difficult to believe that there really are beings whose only food is light, colour, and sound. Human beings would not find light, colours, and sounds sufficiently nourishing, but for creatures who are made of a far subtler, more rarefied matter, they constitute a real force, a power, a true nourishment. But the most important thing to understand is that there is a correspondence between sounds, colours, and perfumes, and the thoughts and feelings of human beings, for our thoughts and feelings produce colours, sounds, and perfumes in the etheric sphere. Here is a whole world waiting to be studied, a vast world of infinite variety and wealth. And it is these correspondences that reveal the basis of all morality and religion.

We can now understand the answer that Jesus

made to the tempter: mankind does not live by bread alone, but by the word of God—that is, by pure colours, harmonious sounds, and subtle perfumes. This was the food Jesus had during those forty days in the wilderness—and indeed throughout his life.

The different states of matter form an uninterrupted continuum, and just as a force can crystallize and become a material form, so too can matter disintegrate and revert to the state of energy.

But let us get back to the example of food. The fruit that we eat is converted into energy, which sustains not only our physical life, but also our mental and emotional life. It is thanks to this energy that we can speak, love, think, and so on. And this shows that we can convert crude forms of matter into subtler forms, and even into light. The reverse is also possible; we can convert light into thoughts, feelings, and food. Of course, only initiates are capable of working this transformation consciously, and this explains how they are able to go without solid food for long periods: they take and condense the light from space, and it becomes their nourishment. This is difficult of course, but it is possible. In some cases you too can do this. In fact you sometimes do so without realizing it. You sometimes go a whole day without eating, simply because you are so busy, and so filled with love that you feel nourished. It is rare, but it does happen. To a lesser degree, therefore, all human beings are capable of nourishing themselves in this way.

All wisdom, all love, every divine thought can be transformed into food, even food for the stomach. This is something that you can corroborate for yourselves.

To the devil's second suggestion—that Jesus throw himself off the roof of the temple, in the conviction that God would send angels to protect him—Jesus replied, 'Do not put the Lord your God to the test.' In other words, you must not try to test the Lord's fidelity and the protection he promises you. This too is very important. So many people think that, just because they belong to a religion or a spiritual movement, they are entitled to special privileges in life and are above the laws of nature or of society. They believe that heaven will protect them whatever they do. But this too is false. The only ones who are 'protected' are those who do not throw themselves off the roof, for those who do so trigger a different law. You are free until you throw yourself off the roof of the temple, but then you become subject to another law and you are no longer free.

Suppose you have a block of stone or a rock perched at the top of a steep slope: as soon as you tip it over the edge, the die is cast; you are no longer free to control its movement. Similarly, until you say the word, until you make a promise, you are free; but as soon as you utter that word, it becomes independent and you no longer have any power over it. In the same way, you are free to give birth to a child, but once it is born it is no longer in your control; it behaves as it pleases— sometimes in opposition to you, who brought it into the world. It is independent because it has its own free will.

Freedom exists only before an action has begun, not afterwards. As soon as we initiate an action we enter a certain realm and are subject to the law of that realm. And that law may tell in our favour or go against us. The second temptation therefore concerns the necessity of behaving reasonably and in harmony with the possibilities that life affords. We can either behave intelli- gently or we can tempt the invisible world. And believe me, you would do better not to tempt it.

To the devil's third suggestion—that Jesus bow down and worship him in exchange for all the treasures of the earth—Jesus replied, 'Away with you Satan! for it is written, "Worship the Lord your God, and serve only him".' This scene is, as it were, a re-enactment of the scene of original sin in the Garden of Eden, when the serpent promised Adam and Eve that by disobeying God they would not only not die, but they would become equal to him. The devil promised Jesus all the wealth and glory of the world if he would adore him, because he wanted to drive a wedge between him and God. He was trying to awaken in Jesus the same spirit of pride that had driven some of the angels to rebel against the Creator.

When he saw that Jesus still resisted him, the devil withdrew. This final failure convinced him that there was nothing more he could do, for once an initiate has overcome the temptation of pride he can no longer be corrupted. Pride is the most difficult of all failings to overcome. It is like the lichen that clings even to the highest peaks of mountains; it dogs the footsteps of an initiate until the very end. So many have fallen a victim to pride—pride in their knowledge, pride in their virtue, pride in their powers. Some have even believed themselves to be the almighty, omniscient God and have risen up against him. But to the temptation of pride Jesus responded with the magical words: 'Worship the Lord your God, and serve only him.'

As we have seen, the three temptations with which the Evil One attempted to corrupt Jesus were in relation to the stomach, the heart, and the mind. Inevitably, each one of you will also be subjected to the same temptations, and in order to overcome them you will have to rely on the three weapons of hope, faith, and love.

Hope is related to the stomach. It is hope that changes stones into bread, for it has the power to transform matter.

Faith is related to the lungs and heart, the temple in which God dwells. When Jesus replied, 'Again it is written, "Do not put the Lord your God to the test",' he was asserting his faith in the Lord who dwelt within him and was refusing to put that faith to the test by the senseless act of throwing himself off the temple.

The third temptation concerns the mind, and this temptation can only be overcome by love. To climb the mountain—that is to say, the peak, the head—is to possess great knowledge, authority, and power. Those who reach this peak are tempted by pride; only their love of God can save them from this temptation.

Hope, faith, and love are the mighty weapons that enable us to triumph over every trial. Hope is the magic weapon against the material vicissitudes of life—deprivation, bereavement, and need. Faith enables us to sense the inner presence of God, to feel sure of his protection without having to put it to the test. Love enables us to be faithful to him and to avoid the sin of pride.

And now I should like to return to a point I touched on earlier: the fact that the beings whom we call devils and evil spirits are actually God's servants, who work to carry out his will. Let me illustrate this. You have perhaps seen a little girl guarding cattle in the countryside. She may be reading or knitting, or just sitting there watching them. At her feet lies a big dog, its eyes fixed on her with devotion, ready to jump up and do whatever she tells it. The wise, well-mannered cows graze quietly, and all is well. But then pandemonium breaks out as one of them starts to bolt into the neighbour's field, and the little girl, who knows what indignation and recriminations this can lead to, sends her dog to bring it back. 'After her.' she tells it. 'Bite her, bring her back.' And the obedient dog races off, barking and nipping at the heels of the cow until she is safely back in her master's field again. And then, satisfied that it has done its duty, it goes back and lies at the young girl's feet again until it has to go after another cow that has taken it into her head to stray. For, of course, the cows have no right to break the law and leave their own meadow, even if the grass does seem to be greener on the other side of the fence. If they break out, the dog goes after them.

Well, this is exactly what happens with the gentleman we call the devil. When human beings break the rules, they get the same treatment as the cows that strayed into the next-door field: the devil goes after them. You will ask, 'Are you saying that we are cattle?' Why not? Human beings have been put to graze quietly in their own meadow; if they break the law by leaving the territory assigned to them and wandering into regions that are out of bounds to them, the dogs are sent to bring them back. And there you have the explanation for our trials and sufferings: they are sent because we have broken the law. If people were pure there would be no reason for misfortune to befall them; but as they are not, as they often break the law, even unwittingly, the dog is sent after them. Yes, for although this dog is very big and savage, it only does what the cowherd tells it to do. And when you become a true servant of God, the dog will still be there, but instead of biting you, it will be at your service too.

So you can be sure of this: the devils themselves and all the spirits of hell are God's servants. Do you imagine that it is the angels who mete out punishment? Oh no, they have better things to do. It is the devils who are sent to torment those who defy the divine order. And as soon as the offenders restore order within themselves and are in harmony once again with God's plan, the devils stop hounding them. This is why God has no desire to destroy these beings; they serve a very useful purpose. They are like insects—they come and clean things up by eating the refuse and impurities that are lying about. But if the impurities are all swept up they will not come back, for there is nothing to attract them.

As long as human beings continue to transgress the divine law, the spirits of hell will continue to torment them. It is not up to the angels and archangels to restore order and teach human beings to behave. They have already tried persuasion and reason, but human beings just dig in their heels and refuse to listen. You cannot expect the angels and archangels, who dwell in absolute harmony, beauty, and perfection, to be responsible for the task of punishing human beings. No, they designate others for this work. And those others obey and carry out their instructions to the letter, because they have promised to do the will of God. And who are these others? They are devils and demons, the 'exterminating angels'. Of course, you will say that in the Apocalypse St John says that it was angels who brought the plagues on mankind. Yes, but those angels were such powerful beings that they only had to make a sign and other forces were set in motion to ravage the earth.

Even sages, saints, and prophets have been tormented by demons who were sent to temper them and make them stronger. These spirits are docile servants; they go wherever they are sent, in obedience to the orders they receive. Those who ravage mankind by means of disasters and disease are not acting on their own initiative; they are the emissaries of those who are responsible for seeing that the laws are obeyed. And as soon as human beings conform with the law again, these spirits are obliged to leave them, for they have to obey those who sent them.

So there you have it. This is the teaching of initiatic science.

Chapter Seven

UNDESIRABLE GUESTS

In the text by the Master Peter Deunov that I read to you this morning there is a sentence that I should like to come back to. He says, 'Evil is like a lodger who comes to your house and stays for years without paying rent.' Some of you will find these words surprising, for not many people are familiar with the idea that a human being is inhabited by foreign entities. And yet it is very important for you to know this. Why is it important? For the sake of three things: your health, your freedom, and your salvation.

Jesus said, 'If you keep my commandments, my Father and I will come and make our home within you.' This means that human beings are designed in such a way that they can give shelter to other entities within their own being. And although these visitors can be the Lord, the Holy Spirit, or Christ, they can also, unfortunately, be demons and spirits of evil. The Gospels make this very clear.

You all know the story of Mary Magdalene, whom Jesus delivered from seven demons. We speak of seven, but as each demon had countless servants with him, they represented a whole legion of undesirable guests. Undesirable? Yes, but to begin with, Mary Magdalene had thought them highly desirable. She herself had invited them and had done all that was needed to attract them. Perhaps you will say, 'But that is not possible. She did not even know they existed.' True, she was too ignorant to know that her way of life, the fact that she lived by seducing men, was a standing invitation to malicious spirits. But once you welcome these creatures, they settle down and expect to be given free board and lodging; they eat and drink, break the furniture and the dishes, symbolically speaking, and lay their dirty hands on everything within you.

When Jesus met Mary Magdalene he saw that she was not an evil woman; she was kind hearted and generous, and it was perhaps because of these qualities that she had agreed to be useful—in her own special way—to so many people. As a matter of fact, if you observe women who have become prostitutes, you will see that they often have outstanding qualities. But at the same time, the poor things are so lacking in intelligence, and so vulnerable and easily influenced, that they become victims. There are always plenty of people who are ready to take advantage of their weakness. And society, too, is very cruel to them.

So Jesus decided to deliver Mary Magdalene from these evil spirits, because he saw that once she was free she would do a great deal of good to other women like herself. Yes, for every being has a special relationship with the other inhabitants of the region or milieu to which they belong. When one falls, many others are dragged down too; and when one lifts himself up, others rise with him. The power of both good and evil comes from the fact that neither of them exists in a vacuum. They both belong to an incalculable network of ramifications, acquaintances, and alliances. This is why all human beings bear a great responsibility in all that they do and think and feel.

You are certainly familiar too with the account of the Gadarene man who was possessed by a devil. When Jesus asked the spirit that inhabited him to tell him its name, it replied, 'My name is Legion', because many demons dwelt in this man and drove him to do all kinds of insane things: he would run naked in the mountains, screaming aloud and slashing himself with sharp stones. But there is no point in talking about all the cases of possession mentioned in the Old and New Testaments. These two examples are sufficient. Esoteric literature is full of tales of how spirits have taken possession of people and tormented and weakened them, until they were eventually destroyed. Also, all religions have rites of exorcism, with special prayers and formulas. From the beginning of time it has been known that a human being is not an empty house, that a great many entities make their home within him.

Undesirable guests therefore are creatures of a lower order who get inside human beings and persuade them to do all kinds of insane and reprehensible things, until they have utterly destroyed themselves. Once a man is inhabited by these spirits he is a prisoner; there is no getting rid of them. Sometimes, by the grace of God, or when someone has already paid his karmic debt and the time for his release has come, his heavenly allies may help him to drive them out. But this is rare, very rare, and in any event, he must earn their help by his own efforts.

Now, of course, if you go and tell people that they have invited malevolent spirits to come and dwell in them, not only will they refuse to believe you, but they will either laugh at you or be very indignant. Unfortunately, though, this is the unadulterated truth. I do not intend to describe these spirits, the forms they take, or the emanations that come from them, because merely to speak about them creates a bond with them. But I want to explain how you attract them: every time your thoughts, feelings, and acts are not absolutely pure, you are creating the conditions these undesirable creatures need in order to infiltrate you.

Take an example from everyday life. If you keep your kitchen table spotlessly clean it will not attract flies or vermin. But if you are careless and leave scraps of food lying about, you will immediately see swarms of little creatures arriving, especially if there are some holes or cracks for them to hide in.

Or take another example. Students of zoology know that each animal species—insects, predators, mammals, reptiles, birds, and so on—needs a particular kind of food. Some eat seeds, others grasses, others meat or worms; and some, such as jackals, hyenas, or vultures, feed on the carcasses of other animals. In order to feed an animal properly, therefore, you have to know what kind of food to give it. And this explains what I have been saying: if you harbour thoughts, desires, and feelings that are neither luminous nor pure, you will be invaded by the kind of creatures who like to feed on these impurities. But if you purify yourself and mend your ways, these entities will go elsewhere, and you will breathe freely once again. You see how clear it all becomes. The pity is that so few people are capable of reading the book of living nature that is open before their eyes. Perhaps you will say that these are only details. They are details, yes, but they have great significance when we see how they apply to our psychic life.

Every thought and feeling that goes through us emits electromagnetic currents conducive either to good or to evil. In this way we can either attract the most luminous and highly evolved beings to ourselves—in which case the other, malevolent creatures are repulsed and consigned to the centre of the earth—or, on the contrary, we attract demons, elementals, and ghosts—and in this case the luminous spirits who had come to help us are driven away by the nauseating stench that emanates from these vile creatures. Unfortunately, no one knows very much about these things, and this ignorance is the cause of a great deal of unhappiness.

As long as the scientific establishment refuses to acknowledge the existence of these invisible creatures and reduces everything that happens in a man to a chemical or physical process, it will not get good results. In reality, as I have already told you, chemical and physical processes are themselves the result of psychic processes; they are no more than consequences. Of course, biologists have never seen one of these objectionable creatures on their scalpels or under the microscope, but that is no reason to deny their existence. The fact that they have never seen them does not mean that they do not exist.

If you only knew the swarms of entities that clairvoyants can see going in and out of human beings and making themselves at home in them. Of course, the people concerned do not see them, but if they were more vigilant, if they were in the habit of analysing themselves, they would be aware of the arrival of a negative entity and would realize where all their inner turmoil comes from. If you suddenly feel unsettled and unhappy, or if you are plagued by vile feelings and desires, it is a sign that some undesirable guests have turned up. And why have they suddenly decided to visit you? Because you have prepared the kind of food that attracts them.

Our physical body is like a house with several different floors, and each floor is fully occupied. The cellar, the ground floor, the first, second, and third floors all have their tenants. And even up in the penthouse are certain inhabitants who have instruments with which to observe the sun, moon, and stars, and who transmit their messages to us. As I have said, human beings can be classed in different categories—brutes, ordinary men, men of talent, geniuses, saints, initiates, and spiritual masters—according to the number and quality of the inhabitants they have attracted into their houses and the greater or lesser degree of harmony that reigns amongst these inhabitants. The phenomenon is very similar to the life of a large family. Nowadays, of course, the extended family does not always live together, but in the past everybody, from the great-grandparents to the great-grandchildren, all lived together in the same house. This is what man's inner house is like.

Sometimes you say, 'I do not know why, but I have the impression that there are two different people in me. When one of them is uppermost I am kind, gentle, and sympathetic, and everybody loves me. Then the other 'me' comes along and I am perfectly horrible.' Well, there are often many more than two who are liable to manifest themselves, but for the moment let us just say that there are two. Neither psychoanalysis nor physiology can really explain the existence of these contradictory manifestations in man. Biologists study the cells of the body, but they know nothing about the inhabitants of those cells. What they are really looking at when they study a cell is someone's house, and they are content to describe its shape—hexagonal, spherical, and so on—and its structure—membrane, protoplasm, and nucleus. They know nothing about the soul that dwells in that house, or about the life force that flows in that soul. And yet it is this that explains all that goes on in man. So, as I say, we are made up of a multitude of inhabitants, all of whom can be divided into two major categories: the good and the bad. And each category manifests itself in turn.

Take a family in which there are two brothers: one of them is a wonderful person, and the other a monster. Naturally, if the parents are good, honest, intelligent people, they are going to be in despair, because they cannot understand where that dreadful child comes from, nor how two brothers could be so different. But it is they who invited both of them. How did they do this? In a previous incarnation, their ignorance of the laws of Karma led them to incur a debt towards someone, and that entity has now come to them to be housed and fed and clothed. So they now have to look after this child, worry their heads over him, and pay for all the mischief he doe .

Each one of us is like a large family with children, parents, and grandparents all living together, and it is truly amazing what you can find out about your inner family if you are observant. Every member clamours to be allowed to speak, gesticulate, and complain in turn, and what they have to say is worth remembering. As I say, they are our responsibility. It is we who attracted them in the first place by breaking certain laws, and now that they are there, it is up to us to educate them. It is extremely difficult to get rid of them; the best we can do is simply to educate them and make great sacrifices for them, because we have a debt towards them.

Of course, these creatures delight in sneaking in wherever they can under false pretences, but it is up to us not to let them in. The spirits of light never go where they have not been invited, but the others have no respect for laws of any kind, so they force their way in without waiting for permission. Initiates sometimes use magic rites and pentacles against these malignant spirits. If you have read Faust (of course, Faust was not an initiate, but he had a certain knowledge of the occult), you will remember that he put a pentagram over the door of his house, in order to prevent elementals from entering and good spirits from leaving. Many different kinds of talismans can be prepared with the help of certain formulas and magic rites, and can be used for our protection. The pentagram is one that is often used by occultists. In everyday life we have notices that say, 'Private property. Keep out', or 'Smoking prohibited', 'Trespassers will be prosecuted', and so on, and the same things exist in the spiritual domain. In the spiritual domain, however, these warning signs take the form of symbols and talismans, and the spirits understand and respect them, whereas the signs that human beings put up are not always very effective. Signs say that you are not allowed to dump refuse, but people go and do it at night. Smoking is forbidden in trains and buses, but nobody pays any attention. But initiates have ways of protecting themselves that are far more effective than these visible signs, and if spirits disobey them they are severely punished.

I wonder if the question is any clearer to you now. People are reluctant to believe in the existence of these undesirable intruders, but whether you like it or not, a great many manifestations and phenomena prove their existence. What is a vice, for example? Nobody would deny that vices are all too real, but how do you explain their existence? Here is a man who is very kind, intelligent, and well-educated, and who has many other good qualities, and yet he also has a terrible vice, which he is powerless to overcome. It is not for lack of trying: he makes heroic efforts, but each time the occasion arises, he simply cannot resist. He may be exceptional in every other area; he may have great talent and be an accomplished musician or artist, but he may also be a confirmed drunkard; he cannot resist a drink. The great singer Chaliapin was like that. What a voice. Yes, but he drank. Others are inveterate gamblers; they will stake their last penny at roulette, baccarat, or the horses. How do you explain such things? Oh yes, people say that someone like that has a complex, or that he caught the habit from his family, or his companions, but that explains exactly nothing.

Official science is not yet equipped to explain these phenomena. Only initiatic science is capable of doing so, and it tells us that vices are beings that a man is obliged to nourish, because it was he who invited them and gave them a home. And there comes a time when he has reinforced them to such an extent that he is completely subjugated and incapable of shaking them off. Yes, my dear brothers and sisters, vices are neither more nor less than creatures who settle down in human beings and enslave them. It is possible to overcome them, to master them, but it requires exceptional will-power and knowledge to do so.

What means should we use in order to avoid attracting these undesirable tenants? The first and most important is purity—purity in every domain—and then heat and light. By means of purity we starve them to death, for where there is purity there is nothing for them to eat. Light terrifies them and drives them away; heat sears and consumes them. Of course, this is a manner of speaking. To possess light is to know things as they really are, and, consequently, to know and understand this whole question clearly. To possess heat is to have an ardent love for a divine ideal. To be pure means to live in an exemplary way that gives these creatures no hold on you, and no opening by which they can sneak in. And if, in spite of everything, they did try to slip in, they would immediately be repulsed, for the qualities of purity, intelligence, and love fend them off.

So, you see, this teaching gives us the elements we need in order to understand these things. It makes it quite clear that it all depends on us, and that, even if we have committed faults in the past which opened our doors to unwanted guests, something can still be done about it. We have to get these creatures to listen to reason and convince them that, instead of ransacking their abode within us, they would do better to help us to embellish it by contributing their talents. If they are musicians, they can give us music; if they are painters, they can paint pictures for us; if they are scholars, they can reveal the secrets of nature to us. For amongst all these creatures there are certainly some who are very knowledgeable and very capable; but as things stand at present, instead of helping us, they drain us of our strength.

When luminous spirits dwell in us, on the other hand, they give us all that they themselves possess. Also, many of these spirits belong to our own family. They are the entities that initiatic science calls 'familiar spirits'; grandfathers and grandmothers who come to help their children and grandchildren. Some of them are altruistic and highly evolved, whereas others are a little less so. When a man has smoked a pipe all his life, for example, he wants to go on doing so through his grandson, and so the grandson starts smoking a pipe too. And because his grandfather is very attached to his pipe and very obstinate, the young man cannot break himself of the habit. Oh yes, you still have a lot to learn.

Some of you may say, 'Oh, all those undesirable guests... I am not interested. I cannot take them seriously.' Little do you know. They are already within you. They already have a firm grip on you. One day you will all have to take this question very seriously. You will all have to learn how to deal with these malevolent entities, how to educate and enlighten them, for, as I say, it is very difficult to get rid of them. In fact, in trying to do so, one can sometimes make matters worse. The solution is to help them therefore, and even to pray for them, and show them great goodwill and much love; otherwise you will only succeed in angering them, and they will devastate you. Only those who are very strong and powerful are capable of driving them out, so before you attempt to do so, the best way is to talk to them and try to reach an understanding with them.

Clairvoyants have sometimes been able to see what happens when people do this. They have seen people who were tormented by an evil entity talking to it, praying for it, or reading it a passage from the Gospels, and they saw that the entity listened and that sometimes it went away. The people themselves, of course, saw none of this; they only felt that their situation had changed for the better, but the clairvoyant actually saw the entity leaving them.

I too have often had the opportunity to verify these things, and as far as I am concerned, there is absolutely no doubt about any of it; I am absolutely convinced. And you too must believe it, or you will never be able to improve your situation. These creatures really do exist. Some of them are quite enlightened and highly evolved and capable of understanding you, but others belong to a lower order, and there is nothing to be done with them. Even when things are explained to them they cannot understand, so you have to use quite different means. And, above all, never try to confront them directly, for, as I have said, it is very dangerous; you will end by being utterly defeated. You must call on other, very luminous and powerful spirits to come and fight in your stead. They are capable of doing so; they have all the weapons they need. You yourself must not engage in combat with them.

As you can see, this is a very vast science, and I cannot explain it all to you in a few minutes, but what I have told you is the essence of it, and if you believe me you will soon be able to make fantastic progress in your evolution.

Chapter Eight

SUICIDE

Fill a glass half full and show it to two different people, asking them to tell you what they see: one will say that it is half full; the other will say that it is half empty. For most people it comes to the same thing, but for those who are familiar with initiatic science, these answers reveal two different mentalities, two different psychological processes. If you dwell on fullness you will feel fulfilled. If you dwell on emptiness you yourself will become empty. This is a law of magic: when a sick person dwells continually on his illness his condition worsens, because negative thoughts have a disintegrating effect. He should think about health, and the thought will make him better.

You may have many needs, but if you want to be even needier, you only have to let your thoughts dwell on all the things you need. If you think instead that you are sons and daughters of

God, and heirs to an immense fortune, you will find that many aspects of your life begin to improve. In any case, the thing that human beings need most is not money, houses, or cars, but a divine, luminous philosophy capable of delivering them from their weaknesses and difficulties.

All this is simple, quite extraordinarily simple. Whatever the circumstances, some people always see the positive aspect of things, while others see only the negative aspects. To be sure, they both see something that is true, but their different ways of evaluating what they see have different effects on them inwardly. As far as the truth is concerned, it makes no difference to say that a glass is half full or half empty; only the magical effect is different. And it is precisely this that is essential. If you are in the habit of seeing all the flaws, defects, and shortcomings of everything, you will become more and more unhappy, discouraged, and embittered. This is the inevitable result of dwelling on what is missing. That there is always something missing is obvious—there is no need to try and convince me of that—but that is not the point. The point is that we must use what we have, in order to advance and improve.

For those who are forever complaining that they have not got this, that, or the other thing—

especially money, for the one thing people complain about most is the shortage of money—I have an argument that should bring home to them just how wrong they are and how much harm they are doing to themselves. I say to them, 'You need money? Very well, I will give you twenty million dollars, but in exchange you must give me your eyes.' Naturally, they would be horrified at the idea. Then I would add, 'And I will give you twenty more for your ears, another twenty for your nose, another twenty for your arms, and another twenty for your legs.' In no time at all my offer is worth billions, and yet they would continue to refuse. But then why do they feel so poor? In fact, they are rich, but they have never realized it. And they have never realized it because they are fools, and fools have to suffer because their head still needs to 'ripen'. It is not I who decide this, it is nature.

Nature is implacable. However much you shout and curse and scream, nature will never change her mind. It is you who have to yield and obey and bring yourself into harmony with her. Yes, nature is inflexible, relentless. Perhaps you think she is cruel. No, nature is not cruel; her one idea is to make human beings more intelligent, more beautiful, and, above all, happier. But what can she do if they are too hard-headed? She has to help their heads to mature, and for this she has her own very effective methods. When she sets to work to change people, she does not explain anything, she simply says to herself, 'I only want what is best for them, and since there is no other way to bring them to their senses, I am obliged to use these methods.' It is not her fault.

You must accept this philosophy, which shows you that you are God's children and heirs to a treasure which will be yours just as soon as you are capable of drawing on it. What human beings lack is a philosophy. Nothing else. They have everything they need, both inwardly and outwardly, and yet they spend their time complaining. They are grumblers, that is all; miserable grumblers. And all because they do not have this divine philosophy. This is why, when I see people curled up inside themselves, concerned only with their own little problems, I feel like telling them, 'Poor wretches, how can you see anything? You never go out; you are locked in your attics. Go out for a walk and have a look at your heritage—at all the forests and mountains, all the rivers and lakes, all the stars—then perhaps you will begin to understand that what you possess is immense. You have everything you need.'

Human beings are like people standing up to their necks in a lake, crying, 'Water, give us water. We are dying of thirst.' They are immersed in the ocean of cosmic light, but their shells are so thick the light cannot pierce it and reach into them. Many, many people in the world today are in this situation. They are always unhappy, always sorry for themselves. Many even end by taking their own lives. They cannot see that it is they themselves who are responsible for the state they are in. Cosmic intelligence has no desire to reduce them to such extremes. It is their own obtuseness that brings them to the point of committing suicide, because they think that life is meaningless. And yet in reality there are still so many unsuspected possibilities in life. There is nothing more stupid than to feel miserable and destitute simply because one is incapable of seeing those possibilities.

But to get back to the glass that is half full or half empty: from a purely objective point of view, as I say, both ways of expressing the fact are equally valid. Yes, but true knowledge is more than the objective perception of facts. True knowledge, true science, is the perception of the consequences in one's own life of this or that fact. When you say that the glass is half full, you are dwelling on the aspect of fullness, and in this way you are accustoming yourself to seeing the positive aspect of things. Even when something unpleasant occurs, instead of watering your garden with floods of tears, you must tell yourself, 'Ah, there are all kinds of possibilities in this situation. Heaven wants me to benefit from it. It is an opportunity to develop qualities that are still lacking in me. Which ones, I wonder...' Then you must try to discover what it is that heaven wants you to learn, and once you have found the answer you will be grateful for the ordeal. This philosophy is very difficult to accept, but it is the best. Once you adopt it, nothing will hold you back. Whatever happens to you, you will continue to advance because you will be reasoning correctly.

Suppose that people are always very unkind to you. All your life long, however good, kind, and considerate you are towards them, they treat you with cruelty and injustice. In the long run you find this so hard to endure that you rebel against the Lord and determine to do away with yourself. But wait. There is something that you have not understood. Why does heaven continually send you the same kind of ordeals? Could it not be that in a previous incarnation it was you who were cruel to others, and now the situation is reversed, because you have to understand just how much you hurt them? Yet you still refuse to see that it is you who are at fault. If you were irreproachable, everybody would be bound to love you and to help and respect you. That is the law. The only

solution therefore is to rid yourself of the
conviction that what you suffer at the hands of
others, which seems to be so flagrantly unjust, is
not unjust at all. These so-called injustices, which
are so real and so visible, are in reality the
expression of an invisible justice. For one reason
or another, you deserve whatever befalls you:
because this is a way of paying your debts; or
because it is the only way to learn certain truths;
or because you need to become much stronger, to
become a genius, a giant, a prodigy.

The one thing that most effectively prevents
people from evolving is the belief that the
difficulties and misfortunes they suffer are an
injustice. They say that fate is unjust, even that
God is unjust, that they deserve better. But how
do they know whether they deserve better or not?
They do not know themselves. They know
nothing about either their past or their present—
and less than nothing about their future. So how
can they judge? Even when a jury convicts a man
of a crime he did not commit—and history has
seen many such miscarriages of justice—behind
this injustice is another justice. Even saints,
initiates, and great masters have been imprisoned,
burned at the stake, or crucified. But the injustice
of their ordeals was only apparent. In reality they
were just, for the twenty-four Elders, the Lords of
Karma, are absolutely just. Their trials were sent

to them either to enable them to pay a debt, or as a way of learning certain truths that they would not have learned otherwise, or in order to spur them on to become ever stronger and more powerful, to become invincible.

Some people think that by doing away with themselves they will escape from their difficulties. The fact is that they will be even worse off in the next world, for none of us have the right to give up before our time has come. To do so is to desert, and the price to be paid will be two or three times greater. There is no room in the world above for those who desert the earth; they will not be admitted, and the time of their suffering will equal the time that remained for them to live on earth.

The attitude of those who take their own lives is truly reprehensible. In the first place, it means that they are ignorant, for they do not know the reason for their trials. Secondly, it means that they are proud, for they think they are better judges of what they deserve than the twenty-four Elders. Lastly, they are weaklings, for they cannot endure their difficulties. So there you have it: ignorance, pride, and weakness. And the invisible world is displeased with people like this who desert their post.

You will say that some people commit suicide because they had an exceptionally exalted ideal, and when they failed to achieve it, they were so disappointed with themselves that they put an end to their life. Yes, but that does not make the act any more legitimate. The one thing that matters most when you have a high ideal is to work to achieve it without fixing a time-limit for its realization. If people fail to achieve their ideal, it means that they were not in possession of the elements of success, and to refuse to admit this and to do away with themselves is nothing but pride. They should persevere.

Most people believe that they are on earth in order to live happily and fulfil their ambitions. No, they are on earth in order to pay their debts, to learn, and to become stronger. This is why heaven cannot have a very high opinion of those who decide to take their own life, for in doing so they put himself above the Lords of all destinies, and the sufferings they call down on themselves are indescribable. This is one of the great truths of initiatic science.

True, the act of suicide can be explained in many different ways, but whatever the reason that makes someone do such a thing, the real reason can always be summed up in a few words. People commit suicide because they do not know that the Creator has placed within them all that they need in order to rise above every circumstance in life: the power to communicate with the beings of the invisible world; the power to create by means of thought; the power to launch their creations into space. They do not know that even in the midst of utter solitude and destitution they need not feel alone and without resources; that they have it within them to feel themselves surrounded by friends and endowed with every imaginable treasure. Whatever befalls us, our inner world is so vast and beautiful that we can always be happy.

Human beings are very ill-informed. They have no inkling of the gifts that God has placed within them, and the least disappointment makes them consider suicide as the only solution. What does this mean? Does it mean that they are such great geniuses, so exceptional that they cannot bear the evil in the world? No, it means that they are poor, miserable creatures bereft of all intelligence, love, and strength; it is their weakness that urges them to take this way out. I know very well that there have been heroic men and women in history who have taken their own lives in order to save an army, a city, or a population, but that is quite another matter. I am not speaking of them; I am speaking of all those— particularly among the young—who drift towards a very bad end simply because they feel alone and misunderstood.

Young people need to know that they possess great wealth. They all have powers of imagination, so what is to prevent them from making use of it? Oh, of course, when they think of their beloved their imagination is fully occupied with kisses and caresses. But why should this precious faculty of imagination, which is a gift from their Creator, be used only for their sensual fantasies? Why should they not learn to use it to call to mind all the reasons they have to feel rich and happy because of all that exists in heaven and on earth... and, above all, within themselves?

The suicides that have occurred in the course of history are too numerous to be counted, but they can all be put into one of three categories. They all stem from a defect of the intelligence, the heart, or the will. If you understand things properly; if you know that there is a divine world peopled by a multitude of glorious beings, and that this divine world has left its imprint on the physical world; if you know that your thoughts and desires are so powerful that with patience and perseverance you can make them come true; and, finally, if you learn self-mastery, and, instead of trying only to gratify your appetites, you envisage all your difficulties as occasions for exercising your will-power... if you do this, believe me, you will never voluntarily put an end to your life. Even privations and destitution, even sickness and solitude will never defeat you; it is you who will triumph over them.

Young people need to convince themselves of at least one thing, and that is that the world is very vast and that they are not alone. The most frequent cause of suicide is the lack of love. When love is lost one wants to die, for without love life is meaningless; life is inseparably linked to love. This is so true. When you are in the arms of your beloved, do you not want to live for ever? Hold tight to love and you will always want to live. Do away with love and you will die. A great many people do away with love, and then they wonder why nothing has the power to interest them any more. The reason is simply that love is no longer present.

When I see a young girl quivering with joy and singing to herself, I know that she has just been with her sweetheart, for that is what love is; love is gaiety. And then, when I see that she is depressed, it is not difficult to interpret the signs: it is because she has lost her beloved. Now you can see why I always insist on the importance of love. Not the kind of love that is all the fashion today—which is, in reality, licentiousness—for that kind of love robs human beings of their reason for living just as effectively as the absence of love.

Yes, the one thing we need to talk about ceaselessly, all our life long, is love, for human beings are still so far from knowing true love, the love that can move mountains and create worlds. Personally, I have found the secret, for I love. I love the Brotherhood. And as long as I love the Brotherhood, all my problems are solved. The Brotherhood is my only interest; I think of nothing else. It is this that gives meaning to my life. If you do the same you will never want to commit suicide.

Chapter Nine

WEAPONS OF LOVE AND LIGHT

Human beings are in the habit of avenging every injury. Every blow received is returned—sometimes twice over. For one kick dealt to them they deal two in return. This instinct of revenge is a residue of the remote past when men were still animals. And in fact, they have still not changed much. Men and women may be respectable outwardly, but what are they inwardly? They still try to get the better of their enemies by using the very weapons that are used against them. If you study what initiatic science has to say on the subject, you will find that it has very little in common with the attitude and behaviour of human beings today.

You cannot overcome evil by evil. You cannot use calumny to overcome those who vilify you; you cannot use jealousy or anger to triumph over those who are jealous or angry. When you use the same weapons as your enemies you put yourself on a par with them and vibrate on the same wavelength, and this makes you vulnerable, for it means that they can attack and injure you from afar. If you want to be safe and invulnerable you must not remain on the same level as your enemy. You must put yourself beyond his reach by rising to a higher level, just as a bird, an aeroplane or a helicopter rises beyond the reach of its attackers. Of course, when I speak of rising I am not saying that you should rise physically, by climbing a tree or a ladder, or by going up on to the roof. To rise means to reach a nobler, purer, more luminous level; to rise to the level of the divine. When you use your will-power to rise to these regions, by means of meditation and prayer, your enemy can no longer reach you. You are protected by your vibrations, which are so different from his. In fact you will forget his very existence.

In any case, you injure yourself by carrying in your mind the image of an enemy, for in doing so you strengthen and nourish it, and it eventually becomes so powerful that it can lay waste to your inner being. Also, you do yourself no good in the eyes of others, for when you continually harp on the subject of your enemies you show them just how vulnerable and vindictive you are. This is a very bad attitude from an initiatic point of view, the point of view of wisdom. Human beings really need to be enlightened on this score. I have never said that you should not do your best to overcome your enemies, but you must find other means of doing so.

When people slander and persecute you, you must rise mentally to the heavenly realms of light. Once you are protected and shielded by light, love, and heavenly power, not only will evil thoughts be unable to reach you, but they will fall back on those who are trying to attack you. This is how initiates, sages, and great masters succeed in defeating their enemies—by the purity, nobility, integrity, and radiance of their lives. Those who emit evil vibrations are always subject to the boomerang effect—the evil they do rebounds on them—but the boomerang effect becomes inoperative if you are just as weak, vicious, impure, and vindictive as your enemies. In this case you cannot help but receive the evil they send you. If you live a life of purity, on the other hand, not only will it be a protection for you, but it will cause all evil, negative vibrations to rebound on those who emit them.

Sorcerers and black magicians achieve their objectives only because human beings are too ignorant and defenceless to resist the evil influences they project. Yes, as long as you are not capable of defending yourself with the weapons of light, you will be in danger. But when such magicians attack an initiate, or one who lives a life of heavenly perfection, they are struck down from above—sometimes even annihilated. If you want to live in safety and be shielded from every attack by word or deed, therefore, your life must change; you must tune yourself to a different wavelength and rise to a higher plane where you will be protected.

In fact, victory can be yours even sooner and more completely if you learn to be more loving and generous. There are people who succeed in rising above all resentment and animosity; they are unperturbed if others hate and slander them and try to ruin them, for they have absolute faith in the power of light. Every day, by means of their spiritual work, they send out rays of light to all creatures, until even their enemies begin to sense their superiority and feel obliged to defer to them. Instead of exterminating their enemies, therefore, such marvellous beings defeat them by their nobility and the magnitude of their virtues, and by the power of light. In this way they win their friendship. And this is important, for you must not forget that even if you overcome your enemies by the usual means—force, subterfuge, or the power of money—this does not mean that your victory will be definitive. Enemies cannot be defeated by such means. They will continue to nurse their animosity towards you. They will never forgive you for defeating them, and one day they will make trouble for you again, either in this incarnation or in the next, for the struggle is not over.

Suppose you do manage to exterminate your enemies; you will only have disposed of their physical bodies. You can never actually exterminate a human being, for each one has an immortal soul and will continue to hate and combat you from the other side. This is why I say that the struggle is not over. It will never be over, for the mentality that has been handed down from generation to generation is archaic, prehistoric, and totally incapable of solving the problem. You are mistaken; everybody is mistaken; whole countries are mistaken in thinking that they can conquer other countries by means of arms, espionage, or economic warfare. One country may well conquer another for a time, but sooner or later those who have been conquered will inevitably rise up and take their revenge. Look at history. Look at the conflicts between France and Germany, Bulgaria and Greece, the Armenians and the Turks... How can such conflicts be resolved? By doing what France and Germany did: they shook hands in friendship and forgot their enmity. If they had not done this we would have seen the Germans taking their revenge, and the conflict would have flared up all over again. Someone has to be the first to offer to shake hands.

It is instinct that urges us to avenge ourselves, not wisdom. If someone hits you, you hit back without thinking. I believe I have already told you about the three yogis who, hoping to attain perfection, withdrew into the forest to pray and meditate. A man came by and hit one of the yogis in the face, and immediately he jumped up and hit him back twice. For him, perfection was still something to be hoped for. The second yogi was also struck and was about to jump up and hit back when an instant of reflection made him sit down again. He at least had learned a measure of self-control. As for the third yogi, he did not even notice when he was hit; he just went on meditating. As you see, there are different categories of human beings. The first yogi belonged to the category of those who still react according to justice—and sometimes to injustice. The second yogi belonged to the category of those who control themselves, because they take the time to reflect. He thought to himself, 'There is no point in retaliating; it will only complicate matters.' The third yogi was so highly evolved that his enemy's blows made no impression on him.

And now I must go even further and say that your enemies are a blessing. You will be thinking, 'The man is out of his mind. How can an enemy be a blessing?' But this reaction shows that you have not understood much about anything. Truly, our enemies can be a blessing, for it is they who help us to become strong and powerful and luminous. It is because you are not enlightened and cannot see this that you succumb to your enemies. If you were intelligent you would understand that they are giving you the opportunity to become a divinity. Your enemies are hidden friends; it is they who oblige you to develop your will-power and to evolve.

It is important to understand that the two principles of light and darkness are always present in the world, and always at war. This means that if you are on the side of darkness you will be attacked by light; and if you are on the side of light you will be attacked by darkness. You have to expect this. Yes, but that is no reason to throw up your hands and do nothing positive. In spite of all the hostility and dissension that surrounds you, you must keep working. And you must keep fighting, but only on condition that you fight with the weapons of light. For as I have already said, if you respond with the same weapons of hatred and cruelty, it means that you are ready to descend to a lower level, to the region in which hostile forces perpetually tear each other apart, and there, of course, you will lose all your strength and all your light. If you sacrifice your strength and beauty and light in order to vanquish your enemies, it is you, in fact, who will be vanquished. And you will also lose your friends, for when they find that you are so much less agreeable to be with, they will leave you alone. What else can you expect if this is your attitude?.

What a thankless task it is to try to explain this to human beings. They are so ignorant that they prefer to destroy themselves by continuing to use all the same old methods. But the methods I give you are so beneficial that, if you understand them, you will always be victorious, always on top of circumstances; for they enable you to use higher energies and forces that are still largely unknown. Enemies are a temptation sent by the invisible world to test you, for your first reaction is to use the arms they use, to prove that you are stronger than they are. They are a temptation, therefore. Yes, but they are also a blessing, for they force you to become stronger. Instead of loafing about in idleness, instead of resting on your laurels, they force you to surpass yourself.

True, this level of consciousness requires great love and goodness, and if human beings continue to avenge themselves, in the belief that it is only right and just to do so, it is precisely because they have not yet developed these virtues sufficiently. The law of reprisal—an eye for an eye, a tooth for a tooth—is still the norm. We are deluding ourselves if we think that the precepts taught by Jesus are applied in the world. No, human beings are still 'giving as good as they get'. Of course, you are free to do as you please, to use whatever means you like to defeat your enemies, but sooner or later you will find out that you have not actually defeated them. Even if you kill them you will not be rid of them, for the laws of karma make it inevitable that you will have to contend with them again one day. If you assassinate your enemy today, sooner or later he will assassinate you, and this pattern will continue until one of you is capable of showing himself to be bigger and more generous by forgiving the other. Only thus will the cycle of revenge be broken. And yet if I were to proclaim these truths before the world, do you think they would be accepted? Oh no, people would take me for a fool. They are too deeply committed to their passions and instincts, to what they call safety, defence, justice, and patriotism. They do not reason; they are capable of expressing only their instinctive nature, and this is not a solution.

Of course, it is harder to improve oneself than to avenge oneself. It takes a great deal of time and effort to work at one's own perfection, whereas it takes no time at all to pick up a gun and shoot someone. And it is this that distinguishes an initiate from an ordinary human being: ordinary human beings always choose the quick and easy solution, whereas initiates choose the solution that takes time and great effort.

It is time to give human beings a new understanding, a new conception of life, capable of releasing them from the hell in which they are imprisoned. Of course, if you want to stay in hell you are at liberty to do so, but if you want to free yourself you will have to learn new methods. Believe me, you cannot defeat an enemy by contempt, violence, or intimidation; there will always be a spark of rebellion in him, waiting for the opportunity to spring at you and take his revenge. If, on the other hand, you use the weapons of love and light, your victory will be decisive, and your enemy, in turn, will love you and be ready to follow you and serve you. All this requires much work and great effort, but you must prize effort and spurn facility, for the path of facility will get you nowhere, and in the long run you will find that in choosing it you have chosen the most difficult.

Chapter Ten

LIGHT YOUR INNER LAMPS

However great your difficulties, you must not wear an expression of gloom or discouragement. On the contrary, you must switch on all your inner lamps, for the more disastrous your situation, the more you need the brightness of those lamps within. And one thing you can be sure of: if you do this, people will come from near and far to ask you if you need anything, if they can help you. Yes, if you light your inner lamps, you will receive so many offers of help that you will not know what to do with them.

As it is, in the belief that your misfortunes interest other people, you keep talking about them, exaggerating them, adding a twinge of pain here and an ulcer there, in the hope of touching their hearts and moving them to help you. But others have only one idea in mind: how to get rid of you as quickly as possible. Yes, I am sorry to have to say this, but it is the truth. People will rarely respond to your lamentations by helping you, because they are not attracted by misfortune; they are attracted by beauty, light and love. The more painful your situation, therefore, the more joyful and radiant you should be.

If you were a better psychologist you would realize that you will never get others to take pity on you by laying bare your trials and sorrows and sufferings. Do not delude yourself—human beings are not compassionate and generous; they are not always ready to listen and respond to the lamentations of those who suffer. Far from it, they like people who are agreeable, poised, elegant, charming, and congenial. If you are none of these things they will want nothing to do with you. It is possible that for appearances' sake they will offer a few words of encouragement, good wishes, or condolence, but in their secret thoughts they will be looking for an excuse to get away from you as quickly as possible. Yes, for better or for worse, this is human nature. If you want to scare people away, keep talking about your illnesses and all your worries and sorrows, and you will soon see how many people listen.

I have known people whose greatest pleasure in life seemed to be to talk about all the most negative and least appetizing details of their existence. And then they were pained and astonished to find that people avoided and abandoned them. What a stupid attitude. It is much better to keep quiet about such ,details. Other people are not capable of helping you to find solutions to your problems, so why talk about them? Not only are you wasting your time by talking about your private life to no purpose, but you lower yourself in other people's esteem. When they see how feeble and unintelligent you are they lose all respect for you and leave you alone.

If you do not want to lose your friends, therefore, hide your troubles from them; do not talk about them, do not complain. Instead, call on the powers above, on all those entities of light that are there, ready to help you. If you do this you will become stronger, more powerful, and more luminous, and the strength and light emanating from you will attract others, for they will see that you are not like everybody else, that you bear your difficulties and trials without complaining. Because of this they will admire you and turn to you in the desire to imitate you and draw strength from you. But if they see that you are always depressed, vulnerable, weak, and pathetic, not only will they have no sympathy for you, but you will be incapable of doing anything to help them.

However great your difficulties, you must always try to find the words that can help others, for it is thanks to this effort of generosity and altruism that you will soon find solutions to your own problems, instead of having to wait for other poor, weak, ignorant people to come to your rescue. And not only that, but when the heavenly entities see the gigantic efforts you are making to advance, they too will come to your assistance.

In any case, you must never resign yourself to feeling gloomy and unhappy without reacting. You must do what you can to pull yourself out of your moments of depression, without, of course, imitating those who resort to artificial stimulants or tranquillizers, for these have a truly crippling effect. The Creator has placed immense reserves of materials and energies in every man and woman. These reserves are hidden deep within us, ready and waiting to be found and used. If we always seek help from outside, our inner forces will remain dormant. Unfortunately, people are particularly passive today, because science constantly reminds them of all the external means it has invented to solve their problems, without realizing that the habitual use of those means has the effect of weakening people rather than of strengthening and healing them. And this is, in fact, what happens; people become more and more fragile and vulnerable. The least little annoyance or mishap knocks them off balance.

Others try to solve their problems by going in for sports or gymnastics. Well, I have no objection to sports—they are all right as far as they go—but your arms and legs alone cannot remedy your inner problems. You cannot arouse the power of the spirit by running races. However great the effort that goes into it, physical means can never solve psychological problems; such problems can only be solved by light.

Instead of allowing yourselves to be submerged by your difficulties, or trying to find all kinds of external remedies, therefore, remember your lamps. Light all your lamps. What lamps am I talking about? Where are they? I am talking about the lamps that God has placed within each one of us from the beginning of time. They come in all shapes, sizes, and colours; and the electric current with which to light them—and which comes from a great distance, from the great power station of the cosmos—has also been placed within each one of us. The trouble is that no one ever thinks of lighting these lamps. No one knows how to do so. And yet it is very simple. On the physical plane you have buttons and switches with which to turn on your lamps, but on the psychic plane you need nothing more than a thought. You only need to think that you are lighting them and they are alight. And do not content yourself with lighting only a few; once you have begun, you must go on and on, until your whole being is brilliantly illuminated.

I realize, of course, that it is very difficult not to give expression to negative feelings of grief, disillusionment, and frustration—and especially of resentment. Whenever someone criticizes or offends you, you immediately have to go and find a friend to whom you can pour out your bitterness. Yes, but then that person in turn feels the weight of your problems and goes and shifts the burden on to someone else. And they in turn shift it on to another, and so it goes on. Your negative feelings are passed on from one to another, until one day they come back to where they began: you.

You must always be very careful about unloading your burdens on to someone else. For one thing, if your words were to reach the ears of those you are complaining about, they might well be even more determined to injure you. It is far better to stop complaining, to put up with your problems and keep quiet about them, and at the same time to light your lamps, by which I mean to become inwardly stronger and more powerful, so as to be capable of transforming and sublimating your anger and distress.

Life contains an abundance of all that human beings need for their instruction. The wise reflect on everything, learn from everything, and make everything serve a good purpose. But those who are unenlightened get no benefit from anything. If something good comes to them, not only do they not recognize the good in it or know how to use it, but they manage to turn it into a stumbling-block. If you are conscious and watchful and learn how to use them, all the difficult moments in your life can contribute to furthering your evolution. Whenever a difficulty arises you will remind yourself that it is an opportunity to become stronger, wiser, and more spiritual; and the more difficulties you have, the stronger you will become. If you were not given these opportunities, you would never develop and grow.

Of course, it is very difficult, and you will succeed only after a great deal of practice. In the meantime, you will fall and pick yourself up, fall and pick yourself up, time and time again, before learning self-mastery and becoming a truly extraordinary being. This is the path, and it is a difficult one, but it is the path of omnipotence.

Books by Omraam Mikhaël Aïvanhov
(translated from the French)

Complete Works

Brochures:

New Presentation

Daily Meditations:
A thought for each day of the year

Audio-cassettes:
KC2510A – The Laws of Reincarnation (2 cassettes)

Editor-Distributor
Editions PROSVETA S.A. - B.P. 12 - 83601 Fréjus Cedex (France)
Tel. 04 94 40 82 41 - Télécopie 04 94 40 80 05
E-mail: international@prosveta.com – Site internet: http://www.prosveta.com

Distributors

AUSTRALIA
SURYOMA LTD
P.O. Box 798 – Brookvale – N.S.W. 2100
e-mail: suryoma@csi.com
Tel and fax (61) 2 9984 8500

AUSTRIA
HARMONIEQUELL VERSAND
A- 5302 Henndorf Hof 37
Tel and fax (43) 6214 7413

BELGIUM
PROSVETA BENELUX
Liersesteenweg 154 B-2547 Lint
Tel (32) 3/455 41 75 Fax 3/454 24 25
N.V. MAKLU Somersstraat 13-15
B-2000 Antwerpen
Tel. (32) 34 55 41 75
VANDER S.A.
Av. des Volontaires 321
B-1150 Bruxelles
Tel. (32) 27 62 98 04 Fax 27 62 06 62

BRAZIL
NOBEL SA – Rua da Balsa, 559
CEP 02910 - São Paulo, SP

BULGARIA
SVETOGLED
Bd Saborny 16 A appt 11 – 9000 Varna

CANADA
PROSVETA Inc. – 3950, Albert Mines
North Hatley (Qc), J0B 2C0
Tel. (819) 564-3287 Fax. (819) 564-1823
in Canada, call toll free: 1-800-854-8212
e-mail: prosveta@prosveta-canada.com

COLUMBIA
PROSVETA
Avenida 46 n° 19 - 14 (Palermo)
Santafe de Bogotá
Tel. (57) 232-01-36 – Fax (57) 633-58-03

CYPRUS
THE SOLAR CIVILISATION BOOKSHOP
73 D Kallipoleos Avenue - Lycavitos
P. O. Box 4947, 1355 – Nicosia
Tel: 02 377503 and 09 680854

GERMANY
PROSVETA Deutschland
Postfach 16 52 – 78616 Rottweil
Tel. 0741-46551 – Fax. 0741-46552
eMail: Prosveta.de@t-online.de
EDIS GmbH, Mühlweg 2
82054 Sauerlach
Tel. (49) 8104-6677-0
Fax. (49) 8104-6677-99

GREAT BRITAIN
PROSVETA
The Doves Nest, Duddleswell Uckfield,
East Sussex TN 22 3JJ
Tel. (01825) 712988 - Fax (01825) 713386
E-Mail: prosveta@pavilion.co.uk

GREECE
EDITIONS PROSVETA – J. VAMVACAS
Moutsopoulou 103 - 18541 Piraeus

HOLLAND
STICHTING PROSVETA NEDERLAND
Zeestraat 50 – 2042 LC Zandvoort

HONG KONG
SWINDON BOOK CO LTD.
246 Deck 2, Ocean Terminal
Harbour City – Tsimshatsui, Kowloon

IRELAND
PROSVETA
The Doves Nest – Duddleswell Uckfield,
East Sussex TN 22 3JJ, U.K.

ITALY .
PROSVETA Coop.
Casella Postale – 06060 Moiano (PG)

LUXEMBOURG
PROSVETA BENELUX
Liersesteenweg 154 B-2547 Lint

NORWAY
PROSVETA NORDEN
Postboks 5101 – 1501 Moss

NEW ZEALAND
PSYCHIC BOOKS
p.o. Box 87-151 – Meadowbank, Auckland 5

PORTUGAL
PUBLICAÇÕES
EUROPA-AMERICA Ltd
Est Lisboa-Sintra KM 14
2726 Mem Martins Codex

ROMANIA
ANTAR
Str. N. Constantinescu 10
Bloc 16A - sc A - Apt. 9
Sector 1 - 71253 Bucarest

SINGAPORE & MALAYSIA
AMERICASIA GLOBAL MARKETING
Clementi Central Post Office
PO Box 108 – Singapore 911204
Tel: (65)892 0503 – Fax: (65)95 199 198
e-mail: harvard1@mbox4.singnet.com.sg

SPAIN
ASOCIACIÓN PROSVETA ESPAÑOLA
C/ Ausias March n° 23 Ático
SP-08010 Barcelona
Tel (34) (3) 412 31 85 - Fax (3) 302 13 72

SWITZERLAND
PROSVETA
Société Coopérative
CH - 1808 Les Monts-de-Corsier
Tel. (41) 21 921 92 18
Fax. (41) 21 922 92 04
e-Mail: prosveta@swissonline.ch

UNITED STATES
PROSVETA U.S.A.
P.O. Box 49614
Los Angeles, California 90049
Tel and Fax (310) 458 3331

VENEZUELA
J. L. Carvajal
Apartado postal - Puerto Ordaz 8050
e-mail: tierra-nueva@usa.net

PRINTED IN FRANCE IN APRIL 1999
EDITIONS PROSVETA, Z.I. DU CAPITOU
B.P.12 – 83601 FRÉJUS
FRANCE

– N° d'impression: 2550 –
Dépôt légal: Avril 1999
Printed in France